Navigati
with Child

Soul healing

NAVIGATING *Anxiety*

WITH CHILDREN & TEENS

A COLLABORATIVE PROJECT BY CASSIE SWIFT

TRUE YOU
CHILDREN'S LIFE COACHING

First Published by True You Children's Life Coaching 2022
Copyright © Cassie Swift 2022

Cassie Swift has asserted her right to be identified as the author of this
Work in accordance with the Copyright, Designs and Patents Act 1988.

ISBN: 978-1-7396179-0-5

For permissions contact:
cassie@trueyouchildrenslifecoaching.co.uk

Editing and typeset by Fuzzy Flamingo
www.fuzzyflamingo.co.uk

Cover design by Heather Hulbert Designs
www.heatherhulbert.co.uk

A catalogue for this book is available from the British Library.

This book is dedicated to all of the children, teenagers and young people's change makers who want to help, encourage and empower our future generation. I see you, and every step forward is a step in the right direction. Our young generation need us to help guide them through their journey into adulthood, navigating the many curveballs they will face along the way. You are appreciated and I hope this book will help you along the way.

DISCLAIMER:

Please be aware that this book contains topics of a sensitive nature, some of which people may find upsetting or triggering.

For permissions contact:
cassie@trueyouchildrenslifecoaching.co.uk

This book is not intended to be a comprehensive medical guide. The opinions and information expressed in this publication are those of the authors only and they are sharing their expertise, but do not represent professional advice. This book is not intended as a substitute for seeking professional medical advice and the reader should regularly consult a medical expert in matters relating to their health, particularly with respect to any symptoms that might require a diagnosis or medical attention. The authors take no responsibility for any actions taken as a result of reading this book and do not assume and hereby disclaim any liability for any losses occurring as a result.

CONTENTS

ANXIETY IS MORE THAN A BUZZWORD

Cassie Swift

"When it rains look for rainbows and when it is dark look for stars."

– Oscar Wilde

Anxiety is a word that is used a lot, and even more so post-pandemic. It's not always used in the right context. Teenagers, especially if there are any feelings of discomfort whatsoever, say, 'It's because of anxiety,' or, 'I suffer with anxiety,' which has come from society's views and definitions of it. Interesting, isn't it?

The Oxford English Dictionary definition of anxiety is 'a feeling of worry, nervousness, or unease about something with an uncertain outcome.' And we are all allowed to feel like that at any time, of course, but especially as a result of the last two years that we have had with the Covid-19 pandemic.

The Mental Health Foundation found that, over a fourteen-day period, 27% of teenagers felt easily annoyed or irritable most days, 26% felt worried, upset or anxious most days and 32% said they had trouble sleeping. (This is from a study during the pandemic in 2021.)

In 2021, it was found that one in six children between the ages of eleven and sixteen had a probable mental health disorder, which went to one in five among young adults aged seventeen to twenty-two. So, anxiety is a really big 'here and now' issue.

There are times when anxiety is completely normal. Children and teens need to know that it's okay to feel nervous – for example, before you sing in front of people or show your artwork or read in front of people – and that is your adrenaline, which can be channelled into anxiety or excitement. This is the same 'anxious' feeling that you get before going on a roller coaster or doing a skydive; it's your body's way of being on edge about something it doesn't know is safe or not, but in these examples it normally turns to excitement.

However, it has become the case that WHENEVER you feel that anxiety, it's negative and everything is going to fall apart. I don't say this lightly as someone who has struggled with anxiety for many years, as I know the fear that accompanies true anxiety.

This book covers several forms of anxiety. The whole reason for this book is to help you and help your children and teens in different scenarios where anxiety can arise. After all, we don't know what we don't know, do we?

I am going to be discussing anxiety related to the question of at what point does anxiety become a problem and lead to behaviours such as 'emotional based school avoidance' (EBSA, often referred to as the extremely inaccurate term 'school refusal'), self-harm and eating disorders, as these are my specialist areas.

As I said, anxiety is a feeling; even saying the word 'anxiety' will cause physical sensations within your body, such as increased heart rate, racing thoughts or shallow breathing. These symptoms can go on to cause panic attacks where everything feels uncontrollable, we don't know what is going to happen or what to do. And at this stage, this negative channelling of adrenaline becomes an issue. Anxiety is a real problem that needs understanding, compassion, help and support.

I believe, through past clients and research – both my own and others – that increased anxiety is due to lack of confidence and low self-esteem. Which brings us to the question: what is self-esteem?

Self-esteem is, put basically, how you value yourself in the world, how you position yourself within the world and how you feel about your self-worth. Now if these are low and you do not value your place in the world, you don't feel like you matter or you don't feel like you're heard, then it is inevitable that you are going to experience anxiety because you have no value of yourself and no feeling of safety within the world you live.

So, in this chapter, I have anxiety in the middle and I have self-esteem to the left, which is what leads to anxiety. What can we work on to prevent anxiety and panic attacks? And then to the right, we have what anxiety can go on to if it is left untreated, if it's dismissed, if we say 'just get over it' or 'pull yourself together': EBSA, self-harm and eating disorders.

We've spoken about anxiety briefly, including what it

is, some symptoms and how it is in danger of becoming a buzzword because of society and social media, as people use it flippantly. But that doesn't make it any easier if your child or your teen is actually struggling with anxiety. If you are unsure if it is true but they keep on saying it, then it is a sign that they are struggling with something and do not know how else to describe it, so it shouldn't be dismissed or ignored, it needs to be looked at. Some questions to ask yourself when your child expresses this feeling of anxiety could be: what are they worrying about? What are they feeling out of control about? We can't ignore these things because what happens is the more that the anxiety is ignored, the more the neural pathways are formed and the fear response is on alert and this goes round as a cycle, with the knock-on effect of continually decreasing self-esteem and self-confidence. And when we have such low self-confidence and self-esteem, that is when we feel totally out of control and we do not know what to do, who we are, where our safe place is, or even where our position in the world is. When this point is reached, there is then a huge need and desire to be able to control something in order to feel safe, which is our body's primary concern; our primitive brain wants to keep us safe and keep us alive and that is when EBSA, eating disorders and self-harming behaviours can begin.

They initially begin with the child or teen being in total control, they control what they eat, they control what they don't eat, they control if they binge, they control if they're sick. They are able to control if they cut themselves, they control if they pull their hair and to some extent they control whether or not they go to school. Soon, though, these behaviours spiral out of control, and the illness takes over, resulting in the unwanted behaviours of eating disorders and self-harm, as well as anxiety and the inability to go to school.

Let's look a little more closely at each of these areas, beginning with eating disorders.

Eating disorders come in many different forms, not just anorexia and bulimia, which are obviously the two most recognised disorders. There is 'binge eating disorder' where a person will eat large quantities of food and not be sick, there is ARFID (avoidant restrictive food intake disorder) whereby people will cut out entire food groups, 'pita' where people eat non-edible items such as chalk, tissue or paper, 'rumination' where people will eat food then bring it back into their mouth and either eat it or spit it out and OSFED (other specified food and eating disorder, which is the new name for EDNOS – eating disorder not otherwise specified). So, as you can see, there is a HUGE range of disordered eating, which develop when a child or teenager is desperately looking for some sort of control over their life that will ease the anxiety that they're feeling and make them feel better about themselves.

Eating disorders are rarely to do with weight and body image but from the need to be in control of something, circling back round to low self-esteem. This then becomes a cycle whether it's eating disorders or self-harming behaviour. It's about catching it in that cycle and changing how you think to enable you to feel more in control of your life and your place within the world.

It is because of this that I am so passionate about delivering this in the early years, helping parents and teachers to know games, activities and tools in which to instil good self-esteem, good self-worth, good self-confidence. It then just becomes an inbuilt response that they don't question. They know that they're valuable, they know that they are deserving and are worthy, which, in turn, decreases anxiety. As a child forms all decisions about the world by the age of seven, the early years are the critical time to normalise and reinforce this sense of belonging. (I have included an activity at the end to help with this.)

I am not saying it will make all anxiety disappear forever, but it will be more of a normalised type of anxiety that you get before performing or going on a roller coaster – those things which actually can be fun.

So, it's important that we start acting on preventative measures for our young people instead of having to be reactive and helping those who can no longer go to school or who have developed an eating disorder, or other self-harming behaviours.

Let's now look at EBSA, often called 'school refusal', which I despise. The reason I dislike it so much is because it gives the impression that a child or teenager is just choosing not to go to school because they can't be bothered and that it's just naughtiness or laziness or any other negative description! In actual fact, it is so, so much more. It is deep-rooted anxiety. And even if your child is 'playing up', not listening to them and trying to push them is not going to help. We can scream and shout and moan and all it will do is disconnect, break down and even destroy our relationship, which is the last thing we want, as that then reinforces their worth in the world and breaks the often only safe space – home and family – that these young people have, which is a very dangerous place to end up; despair and loneliness never equal a happy outcome. A more accurate description is EBSA, which is emotionally based school avoidance; it is emotionally based not behaviour based and these emotions are worse when in school, so it is a better phrase than just school refusal.

So, what are some of the causes of school anxiety? There is an unending list but some things may include: starting or moving to a new school, friendship difficulties (which is VERY common among teenagers), hormone changes, not fitting in, exam or academic pressure, bullying, grief, bereavement, loss of a pet, unwell parents. There are so many things that put together lead to an overwhelming anxiety of just wanting to avoid the place where they experience this discomfort and intense negative feelings.

One way in which our children and teens will show they do not want to go to school is seeking the comfort and security of home. Remember, we have been told for the past two years we have to stay at home to keep safe; our children don't forget things like this. They will prefer to remain close to parental figures and, when that separation occurs, the child will display emotional upset. There may be real but unexplained physical symptoms at even the thought of going to school, for example tummy ache, headache or feeling sick. There may be clear antisocial tendencies, not wanting to interact or even hold eye contact with others and they don't try to hide the problem either. The behaviours will differ with age, so younger children may fear abandonment, may not feel safe with teachers or be scared of being bullied. Older children may be more concerned about academic performance, changing for gym in front of others or having to perform in front of people. All of these are extremely valid fears and worries when you are only a child or teenager with limited knowledge about the world and how it works.

There are many ways in which we can support our children and young people in this situation, but you do have to be strong for your child, to be able to stand your ground and stand by what is best for your child. The first thing I would encourage you to do is to notify the school and to get a clear channel of communication open. If it means them having some time off school whilst you sort things out, then that is what has to happen. There's no point sending a child to school if you are fighting and arguing and they are stressed and upset, as they will not be able to learn anything, anyway. The next thing I would do is contact your GP and get a letter of support stating they are not able to attend school currently, similar to what adults have as sick notes to give to their employer. This 'proves' that this is a medical condition and not simply a refusal to go to school.

When they are in school, having a toilet pass to avoid the busyness at break and lunch, having a pass to leave lessons five minutes early and going to lunch early – again avoiding the mad rush at these particular times – can really help them. Getting everything prepared before they go into school and setting a clear routine so things are that little bit easier and less overwhelming means there are fewer things to worry about.

When they are not at school, try and get them to have some down time, teach them about self-care and the importance of looking after themselves. You can also have a journal in which you could write prompts; they can just write about things that are coming up and then you can work through them in various different ways. The Box of Hope™ can work in a very, very positive way, not just for those who self-harm, but also for any type of anxiety, as it provides a distraction in which to regulate and ground again, reducing the risk of panic attacks or self-harming behaviours.

Which brings us on to self-harm. This is a behaviour in which your child or teen will intentionally hurt themselves by anything from hair pulling, cutting and burning to taking drugs or having unsafe sex. This happens when things have spiralled so far out of control your child has no self-esteem left. The first thing to do is to seek professional help, take things slowly and really listen to your child or teen. Secondly – this sometimes surprises people when I say this – have a fully stocked first aid kit with everything including Steri-Strips and burn coverings. Recovering from self-harm is a long process and there will be setbacks, so ensuring the wound is clean and does not get infected is of paramount importance.

As your child becomes more aware of what triggers the self-harming behaviour, the 'power of the pause' is so important. There is a ninety-second timeframe in which adrenaline will continue to rise and this is where things like panic attacks, bingeing or self-harming can happen. After this ninety-second period, the adrenaline begins to fall and the risk of unwanted behaviours reduces dramatically. It is so important to be able to pause and distract our child during this period and this can be done in a number of ways, but my favourite and top recommendation is to create and use The Box of Hope™.

The idea is to put things into the box that have a personal, safe and happy connection, as well as distraction tools. So, for example:

- Photos of family, friends, pets, holidays.
- USB with favourite songs, hymns, or background/ white noise.
- Fidget toys.
- Nail varnish or hand cream.
- Essential oils.
- Comforting perfume.
- Favourite chocolate bar.
- Popping candy (sensation).
- Bottle of water (slow breathing down).
- Journal affirmations.
- Breathing techniques.
- Mindful colouring pens and pencils.
- Positive letters, either from other people or yourself.
- Emergency phone number list in case you need to

speak to someone but find yourself on your own.
- Anything else which is special to you (avoid anything that needs a lighter or pencil sharpener or anything that could cause harm).

Just getting past the ninety-second time period is the main aim, as this allows for adrenaline to subside, along with the urge to self-harm.

Validate and listen to them and try to keep calm. There's no point shouting at them as they will not take anything you say in, as they will shut you off. Do you listen to someone when they are shouting at you? It works in exactly the same way.

There are many breathing techniques, including my variation of box breathing, in which you breathe in for one side of the box, out for another and continue until breathing is slower. Finger breathing is where you breathe in and you trace up one side of the finger and then breathe out as you trace down the other side and you continue this for all the fingers.

It is important to celebrate and recognise every single small achievement and do that for yourself as well. Getting ready for school, even if they're late: they have got up and got ready, so celebrate it; let them know you can see how hard this is for them but how well they are doing. It will not always be perfect, but you celebrate the good, you work on the not so good and just try to support them as much as possible. If they are at home, try to get them to do something they enjoy and try to get some fresh air; fresh air and bare feet allow grounding. Screen time is difficult but try to set some boundaries. Let them know you are there and that you won't judge them. Reassure them they are safe, and you've got their back NO MATTER WHAT HAPPENS EVER! You won't love them any less for messing up and you are 100% there for them.

Please remember, in all of the above situations:
- Be kind to yourself and your child.
- Reach out for help and support as there are people who can help.
- There is no quick fix, so allow space to just be with one another.
- Try to encourage speaking about feelings and emotions; do not push or rush, as this can cause relapses.
- Know that you are not alone, there is ALWAYS someone there for you.

★★★

To all those who are on the journey of equipping our children and young people for adulthood, know you are doing your best; there is no manual and having this book shows you want a different way of doing things! Remember you do not know what you do not know, be kind to yourself and celebrate those wins along the way! You have got this!

Cassie has been described by her children as 'awesome,

kind, incredible, caring, beautiful, and AMAZEBALLS'. Her friends describe her as a kind-hearted, loving and courageous woman and single mother of three. She will stand up for her beliefs and the rights of others. Cassie experienced bullying throughout her entire school life, and wishes that there had been someone available to have turned to, because as a result, her mental health deteriorated. This is not something anyone would wish for a child, and no one deserves to feel this way or experience what she went through.

Cassie works as a family empowerment guide, specifically for teens, to enable them to feel empowered about life; she helps them to manage big emotions in a positive way, accepting the true version of themselves. As a result, she brings calm and happiness not only to those she works with, but to the whole family.

Cassie is also a #1 best-selling author of four books, founder and organiser of the Children's Mental Health Matters Summit, and she has appeared on the radio and in six local newspapers speaking about issues surrounding children's mental health.

"Helping others, especially children, is my passion. I want to empower as many children as I possibly can!"

https://linktr.ee/CassieS

Listen to the audio version here:
https://bit.ly/Anxietyismorethanabuzzword

THE IMPACT OF OUR LANGUAGE ON ANXIETY

Kari Roberts

"If the only thing people learned was to not be afraid of their experiences, that alone would change the world."
– Syd Banks

Anxiety is something that is felt by everyone. It is a very human emotion but very rarely talked about openly and honestly, whatever age we are. There is so much talk about anxiety and it is so important to understand what impact the language we use can have on it. Unintentionally, we can make the feeling more intense. We can build fear, guilt, shame and misunderstanding that stays with us and intensifies anxiety until it starts to control us. First of all, knowing anxiety is an internally pushed emotion warning us of a perceived threat may help us to understand how to help our children when they feel anxious. This is key. Why is this so important, you might ask? Anxiety is at the very beginning of the mental health continuum. We can become emotionally stuck in our anxiety and this can then lead to other mental health issues. Starting here can stop us travelling down the continuum.

I think of anxiety like my internal alarm clock, letting me know when there is something that I am worried about, something that may be unsafe or different. It doesn't mean it's real, it's just my body's way of saying something doesn't feel right. Ignoring it means the alarm clock will keep going off. Snoozing it will stop it for a while, but it will just be waiting to go off again. The only way to stop the alarm is to wake up, switch off the alarm and check in with how I am feeling. Asking myself:

- What is the threat?
- Is it real?
- If I think it is real, what facts do I have that it is real?
- Is this going to stop me getting up and on with the day?
- Am I thinking of what if, rather than focusing on what is?

I remember when I was teaching emotional literacy over twelve years ago with primary aged children, the word 'anxious' was not widely used. They understood the word worried but not anxious. Now the word is used everywhere and mostly seen as the emotion to avoid and not feel. Feeling anxious is part of being human. Anxiety is one of the very first emotions humans had that did not have a name. It was a gut feeling, a response to the environment around us to keep us alive. It was to push us to take notice, to make sure there were no wild animals or enemies to kill us and was key for our survival. Over the years, as society has developed, we do not need to be that alert every day. However, it has stayed with us, in our core DNA, even though we do not need to be constantly looking for danger.

Sometimes children can be seen as angry rather than anxious and this develops a lot of misunderstanding by the adults around them. This misunderstanding can then escalate their behaviour. When our children show emotions through behaviour, correction tends to be used; yes, they may be unpleasant to feel and to witness being felt, but they are not bad. If you correct the child while they are feeling these strong emotions, you are not connecting with them and they start to disconnect from adults around them and think there is something wrong with them, when in fact they are just being human. How would you feel if you were shouted at, ignored or punished for saying how you felt? Connection is key to long-lasting stable relationships.

Think of an iceberg: above the waterline is what we see, the behaviour, which can be shouting, fighting, swearing, withdrawing, sometimes being overly focused to name just a few. Now let's look at what is pushing that behaviour under the waterline: fear, grief, a sense of loss or shock, which could be connected with world events, home life, school or friendships. One thing that may help is to put all these categories into a physical box. Name the box. Close the lid, then when you feel anxious about that particular thing, take the box, open it and look at that individual worry.

Ask these questions:

- What is the story I am telling myself about this?
- Do I know this story is real?
- How do I know it's real? (Because I think it is or

because it happened before does not mean it's real!)
• What could the story be instead?

Close the lid and then put the box to the side. It can be revisited as many times as needed but each time the intensity of the feeling will lessen.

To help our children develop a healthy relationship with their anxiety, the adults around them have to first develop their own healthy relationship with it.

As previously mentioned, language is important when we talk about anxiety. There is a myth that anxiety is a 'bad' emotion, when really it is one of the most important human emotions. Realising there is a big difference between someone 'feeling anxious' and 'being anxious' is huge. We can get overwhelmed with messages about what is good or what is bad, how we should behave, look and respond to others. Most of us would have used avoidance as a default: don't feel the feelings, that is a bad feeling. This works for a while but then avoidance becomes part of the anxiety, thinking it goes away, but as science shows, it just festers and marinates away in our bodies, seeping out in other ways like stomach issues, aches and pains, headaches and sometimes catching us unaware with a massive explosion of emotion! Have you ever seen someone shake a bottle of fizzy drink and then take the lid off? Your emotions are like that, they build and build until they explode, normally resulting in being told off or others saying we overreacted.

When we feel anxious, our brains will automatically feel it needs to protect ourselves and cannot tell the difference between a situation that is dangerous for us or something we just feel uncomfortable about. Anxiety increases energy levels preparing the body for fight or flight. Adrenaline rushes around our bodies. If harnessed, this adrenaline can be really useful, for example if we are running a race or going on stage to perform, but if we continually release this adrenaline without using it, it will just leave us feeling on edge and exhausted.

Recognising signs of anxiety before nervousness and other symptoms of anxiety get out of hand can help you reduce the intensity.

Typically, anxiety symptoms can fit into one of three categories: physical, thought and behaviour. Take time to answer how anxiety may affect you in those three ways.

Here are a few examples of how anxiety shows in both adults and children:

Physical

Tummy ache
Chest pains
Difficulty breathing
Feeling dizzy, lightheaded
Headache
Needing the toilet
Muscle ache
Feeling sick
Blurry vision
Energised

Thoughts

Not able to concentrate or think
Erratic
Can't get to sleep
I feel unwanted
I feel sad
I am not good enough
Feeling on edge
A lot of 'I can't do' thoughts or 'this is unfair'
Low self-esteem
Focused obsessively on something
Questioning

Behaviour

Hitting out or shouting
Fidgety
Withdrawn
Controlling
Impulsive
Short-tempered
Crying
Frantic
Smiling when people watch
Saying 'I am fine' all the time

When we talk to our children about anxiety, it is important
to remember not to assume they are thinking the same thing

you are thinking. When I worked as a youth development officer, I would sit in meetings with adults assuming what young people were thinking and developing services around that. What young people really thought was very different and the most successful services were those that listened to them and didn't make assumptions. It can be really uncomfortable as an adult to hear our children say they feel worried, or if they say they feel unwanted, or lonely. Saying things like 'oh don't worry about that' or 'that is silly' may give them the message that what they are feeling is wrong or not to talk about it as no one understands. Another thing adults tend to do is panic about what help is needed and flood the child with help. This is overwhelming and often can cause the person feeling anxious to withdraw, feel more anxious and scared to talk about it. Anxiety can be infectious, so check in with how you are feeling. Sometimes even hearing the word makes us feel anxious!

Some useful narratives to use for both us and our children are:

"I can see how anxious you are" – when children are anxious, trust there is no need to fix it and make it better, just listening to them will help.

"I totally understand why you are anxious"

"It's okay if you don't know what you're anxious about"

"Do you want me to help?"

Sometimes children or adults may not be able to tell you what they are feeling. Remember, developmentally, under fives cannot naturally regulate their emotions and they need the adults around them to help, therefore checking in with your own emotions is crucial.

An emotions diary can help anyone to check in on their emotions every day. There are some great ones on the market, however they are very simple to make, and it is a great activity to do with children of any age. If you are creative then draw the emotion in the way that makes sense to you; you can download different emojis or expressions from the internet. The trick is to keep it simple. Just have the words I feel and then space for the emotion. Sometimes just naming it helps.

As you use it more and more then you may feel like writing more.

For example:

I feel ………

when …………

because ………

What I want is ………

But start with very simple steps. Overcomplicating things is the main reason to stop doing it.

Another useful tip is to develop an emotional treasure box/toolkit. Create a physical box of things that can help. Here are some things that you could include. Remember things that help will be different for everyone. Some things that calm me may not calm others.

- Bubbles – blowing bubbles will help regulate the breathing
- Balloons – another breathing technique
- Colouring books

- Music – either just to listen to or dance to. Why not create a playlist?
- A blanket or toy that your child chooses that calms them
- Fidget toys
- Beaded bracelets

Anxiety is a really useful emotion and, if we and children understand what it is and how it shows up, giving them the tools to manage it will help them start to be able to regulate it and see it as a friend who reminds them sometimes to check in and make sure it's safe. The whole basis of what I have learnt through emotional science is that every emotion is valid and has a useful purpose. It acts as an alarm clock, highlighting something different. How do you feel confident and safe without letting anxiety be felt?

Some of you may be fortunate enough to have been taught to express your feelings fully but sadly that is not the case for many of us. I see so many that have had years of conditioning and I believe we have to stop this narrative around emotions, especially anxiety. Feeling anger or frustration doesn't make anyone a bad person; in fact, it is part of being human. So, what is the fear of raising a generation that is secure with who they are and fully understand, know and respect their emotions? How wonderful to feel each emotion without judgement or shame. Let's make this change one step at a time!

★★★

I dedicate this chapter to my granddaughter Honey, for her courage to feel her anxiety and not be afraid to make friends with it, teaching me more than I ever imagined.

Kari is a specialist parent coach. She works to build parents' confidence to parent in the way that works for them and their children, without breaking anyone's spirit. With over fifteen years of professional and thirty-seven years of personal experience, she knows that what children need is for the adults around them to be secure in who they are and be emotionally healthy.

★Start with you and then things for your children will fall into place!★

https://linktr.ee/kariann2309

Listen to the audio version here:
https://bit.ly/impactoflanguage

DECREASING ANXIETY AND INSPIRING YOUNG PEOPLE TO SHINE BRIGHTLY

How leading with compassion, kindness and responsiveness in our relationships with children can decrease their levels of anxiety

Beckie Shuttleworth

> *"If we make it a priority to build relationships in which children feel safe, we have a good chance of reducing children's and young people's levels of anxiety and increasing their sense of well-being."*

Anxiety can be defined simply as worrying about the future or the unknown. For children and young people, because they have had less life experience than adults, so much is as yet unknown. What might seem obvious to us is, in fact, the complete unknown to them.

For children, every moment is a learning opportunity. They are constantly taking in new information and having so many of their life's 'firsts'. It's to be expected that they won't always learn things the first time they encounter something new, and with many new skills they will need lots of practice.

Traditionally, much of the advice available to parents and the systems created in educational settings do not support the development of the type of secure relationships which promote the lessening of anxiety.

The aim of this chapter is certainly not to make anyone feel bad for not knowing, because to paraphrase Donald Rumsfeld, you don't know what you don't know. In the wise words of Maya Angelou, you 'do the best you can until you know better. Then when you know better, do better.'

Young people today face increasing pressures and expectations both academically and socially, as well as facing a future of climate change. The far-reaching impact of the global pandemic has for many young people exacerbated their anxiety and large numbers of young people have struggled with aspects of their well-being since the outbreak of COVID-19.

In addition, the 24/7 nature of the twenty-first century means that many of us, young people included, are always contactable. Use of mobile phones, messaging apps and social media means that we are in constant contact with others and that young people are bombarded with messages about themselves. They learn to rely on approval and validation from the outside rather than from within and expectations can be completely unrealistic. This can be a driving factor in anxiety and other aspects of mental ill health.

So, maybe a new perspective is needed to make a change, because if nothing changes, nothing changes. And something has to change. The things that we can change most easily are the things we have control over, and one of those things is our own interactions with the young people in our lives.

As humanity explores equity for marginalised groups, such as women, black and brown people and those on lower incomes, through movements such as feminism, the civil rights movement and Black Lives Matter, the 'childism' movement suggests it's also time for us to examine the ways in which we, often unwittingly, disadvantage and disenfranchise children and young people.

The concept of childism recognises that young people are 'often disadvantaged compared to adults. And so, it strives to change societies in ways that better respond to children's actual lives' (The Childism Institute, *Childism: An Introduction*).

As leaders in our families and in educational settings, we are in the position to have an impact upon every child we come into contact with. One of the aspects of marginalisation that childism asks us to explore is the way in which adults communicate with children.

As you will know, you can't be made to feel better when something goes wrong by being made to feel worse. For example, being told when something goes wrong, 'If you'd been listening, you'd have known that would happen,' doesn't help when you're already feeling bad. It's important that we support children in feeling safe even when they've made a mistake. A more helpful response might be, 'Oh, you were running and you fell over. I can see that hurt. Are you okay?'

If we make it a priority to build relationships in which children feel safe, we have a good chance of reducing children's and young people's levels of anxiety and increasing their sense of well-being.

Creating an environment where they feel safe and accepted can have a dramatic effect on well-being, as illustrated by a peer-reviewed study published in *Transgender Health*, which found that 'acceptance of one's gender identity from adults and peers was associated with significantly lower odds of attempting suicide' (The Trevor Project). Whilst this study is looking at the extreme impact of non-acceptance for transgender youths, I would suggest that acceptance by trusted adults and feeling safe could be a driving factor in improving well-being and decreasing anxiety for all young people.

Remember that all behaviours are nothing more than a need expressed while emotions are running riot in a child's body, and that they haven't yet learnt other ways to express them. Unfortunately, we have often failed to understand this need, and children expressing emotions in ways that adults find challenging have historically been portrayed as attention-seeking and even manipulative.

But we know that anxiety stems from feeling unsafe. And if those who are entrusted to care for us don't show compassion and respond to needs, how can we feel safe? When we don't take the time to listen, believe and then respond to what the children show us through their behaviour, we are missing opportunities for connection and the building of trust.

For many years, the prevailing advice given to parents and educators has been to separate children from others if they display behaviour that is challenging by giving them 'time out' or to ignore certain behaviours. But separation and planned ignoring can be damaging. When we ignore behaviours that express needs, we can inadvertently teach the child that their feelings don't matter enough to be responded to.

If we consider that, every moment, children are learning how to be in the world from observing interactions between people and from their interactions with other people, we can begin to understand the importance of feeling compassion for them and responding with kindness before anything else.

Could it be that this approach is, in fact, the most important aspect of the way that we care for and educate children? I believe so. It's these elements, the cornerstones of gentle and conscious parenting and educating, that will invite the children into our lives to flourish and shine brightly.

Children of 'highly responsive parents trust that their parents will meet their needs. As a result, they are less stressed, soothe more easily and have more appropriate emotional responses'. Through this trusting relationship built on responsiveness, children develop secure attachments, which allow them to develop a 'plethora of positive development outcomes', including being 'calmer, more engaged and [displaying more] independent behaviour'.

'Children benefit from predictable, loving, compassionate care' (Alana Pace, *Parenting from the Heart*).

In *The Power of Showing Up*, Siegel and Bryson discuss the importance of the four S's that children need to cultivate a healthy emotional landscape. They need to feel not only *safe*, as discussed here, but also *seen*, *soothed* and *secure*. This is where being responsive to their needs from a place of compassion comes in. Ultimately, children need to know that nothing that they could do could make you love them any less. Through this modelled behaviour, they also learn how important it is for them to be compassionate and kind and responsive to themselves and to others.

While children learn and develop ways in which to express their experiences in ways that are considered socially acceptable, the role of the trusted adult is to ensure that the child feels safe. Feeling safe is a multi-layered experience comprising the body, mind and soul. We can support children in feeling safe by holding space for their feelings and their understanding of their experience of the world. If we want children to grow up to be valued and important contributors to their society, we must empower them to practise this as young people. We must listen with compassion and respond with kindness.

We also get to treat children with the same respect and dignity we treat adults, modelling kind and respectful behaviour in all of our interactions with all beings. We get to include children in decisions that affect them and foster an environment of open communication.

In my well-being programme for young people, SHINE Brightly, we cultivate a BRAVE space in which we value:

- **BOUNDARIES** – we can tell each other what is okay for us and what is not.
- **RESPECT** – we respect other people's boundaries and opinions, we listen when they speak and we are respectful with our words.
- **ALL** feelings and emotions are valid and valued. It's okay to be sad, angry, nervous, worried, as well as happy!
- **VOICE** – when we need help or want to ask a question, we communicate with each other by speaking, writing or drawing.
- **EXPLORE, ENRICH** and **EXPAND** – sometimes the work we do together can feel hard, change can be challenging, but we are **BRAVE**.

In our BRAVE space, we know that sometimes being BRAVE is feeling the fear and doing it anyway, and sometimes it's saying 'this isn't for me right now, I'm going to sit this one out'. We can listen to what feels right for us, respect that feeling and communicate it to others.

BIG feelings – they are not just for children! How you can support your child (and yourself) when things are getting too much

As with adults, when children are thrown off balance by a situation and they are already in their BIG feelings, it can be hard for them to engage with something new. I really recommend making these practices part of everyday life when things are calm, so that they are embedded in your family's toolbox for the times you need them most!

BREATHE

Connecting to our breath is fundamental to our well-being. The breath is a tool that is always with us. Most of us will have rarely consciously paid attention to our breath. For the vast majority of us, breath just happens. But breath that just happens is not the same as conscious breathing!

Conscious breathing has the power to change the messages that our body and brain send to each other, helping us to feel safer and calmer at times when stress threatens to overwhelm us. Sharing with children the power that their breath holds is truly one of the most empowering tools we can give them.

Hand to chest and tummy – Sit or stand with one hand on your chest and one hand on your tummy. Inhale and exhale through your nose. Notice the breath flow through your body. See if you can keep your chest quite still. Notice your tummy rise and fall with the breath.

Five finger breathing – Put one hand out in front of you as if you are giving a high five. Take the first finger of the other hand and, as you breathe in, trace up the side of your thumb. As you breathe out, trace down the other side of your thumb. Repeat for each of your fingers. You have done five conscious breaths! Repeat on the other hand.

Blowing out the butterflies – When you have flutters in your tummy, or you are feeling nervous or worried, imagine butterflies of all colours of the rainbow in your tummy. Take a big breath in through your nose and, as you blow the air out through your mouth, imagine all the red butterflies are flying away. Repeat this for orange, yellow, green, blue and purple, and finally, with one last long, slow, deep breath, blow away any final little butterflies you missed the first time. Do you feel calmer now?

Use **these links** to access the three breathing exercise videos I made for you and your child:
- Blowing away the Butterflies: https://bit.ly/blowing awaybutterflies
- Five Finger Breathing: https://bit.ly/Fivefingerbreathing
- Hand to Chest and Tummy Breathing: https://bit.ly/ handtotummybreathing

INTEND/INTUITION

After you've practised a few conscious breaths, check in and see:
- What is the intention here or what are you or your child trying to achieve?
- What is your intuition telling you/them? What do you/ they need?

GROUND

Grounding happens when we put our skin in direct contact

with the surface of the earth or the solid surface underneath us.

When we are grounded, we feel still, present with our bodies, connected with the earth below us.

When we are grounded, we feel more centred and balanced, even when there are lots of things going on around us.

One Minute Grounding Activity!

- While standing, become still, and feel the earth beneath your feet.
- Begin to gently rock back and forth from your heels to your toes and then from right foot to left foot.
- Then come to stillness and take a few long breaths in through your nose and out through your mouth.
- Focus on the feeling of the earth beneath your feet and the breath as it moves through your body.

This activity is suitable for children and adults and, if you can do it outside with bare feet, even better!

Go to this link for the video I've created to show you exactly how I do it: Grounding Exercise: https://bit.ly/groundingexercisevideo

These steps in this exact order may not be a perfect fit for every child every time. Sometimes your child may need you to hold them until the tears slow. During this time, if you are breathing slowly, steadily and deeply, your child will feel your calm increasing, and your energy will support them. Sometimes your child might want to be given space to get all their feelings about a situation out. That's okay. You can support them by being there and holding the space. You could say 'it feels really good to get all that out, doesn't it?'

Remember that you know your child best, and you can pick and choose from these activities depending on the situation. As children become more familiar with using these activities, they will also be able to pick what's right for them in the moment. They will become more independent at managing their emotions, which is ultimately the goal.

And when those times arise when things could have gone better, which inevitably will happen, once everything has calmed down, we get to talk to the children and young people in our lives about how we could have done things differently, so we can learn together.

Children don't need us to be perfect – they need us to be compassionate, kind and responsive.

★★★

To all the souls who long to be in a world that responds to every being with compassion and kindness, all those willing to explore new ways of doing things, and of course to my own parents for being the first people to give me this gift.

Beckie is the founder of Bhumi Yoga and Bhumi Kids and is a children's well-being mentor and childhood specialist. She also shares yoga and meditation with children, adults and families. She holds a first-class honours degree in education and early childhood studies and a PGCE. She has twenty-five years' experience of working with children and their families in schools, out of school care, children's centres, early years settings and their homes.

Beckie is a qualified adult and children's yoga teacher, reiki master, forest school leader and EFT for kids practitioner.

Beckie's vision is that, through her holistic well-being programme SHINE Brightly, all children will come to understand that they are perfect, whole and worthy of all that they desire, and they will be inspired to SHINE Brightly as their most authentic and joyful selves.

She is based in London and offers both online and in-person services.

https://linktr.ee/bhumibeckie

Listen to the audio version here:
https://bit.ly/SHINEBrightly

SOCIAL MEDIA AND ANXIETY

Charlotte Lewington

*"Yesterday is but a dream
And tomorrow is only a vision but today well lived makes
every day yesterday a dream of happiness and every
tomorrow a vision of hope."*

– Francis Gray

I remember the very first day that I was introduced to social media. It all started with a networking platform called MySpace, which was like a basic version of Facebook, and then later on Instagram was created. It is crazy to think just how many social media platforms there are now and the way it has advanced in such a short space of time.

At first, I thought it was a great way to connect with other people. I loved that you could post photos and stay connected to people anywhere in the world. At the time, I was involved in a new business project and thought it would be a great tool that I could use to grow my business. I have always had a love for people; listening to their stories and finding out what makes them tick is something that I enjoy doing. I also love to travel, so seeing everyone's photos of their holidays and gaining different ideas of where to go seemed such a good idea.

There are still many positive outcomes of using social media, but there are also some risks to teenagers' health that parents and professionals need to be aware of. We all have a duty to learn what is happening. Even if you want to abstain from social media, it is important to learn the language so that you can educate the young people in your life on safe practices.

In today's society, social media has been increasingly used to connect with others, consume content and share information. Consistent with the growth of social media use, there are also increasing worries that social media might lead to social anxiety. Many studies have indicated that social anxiety could arise from managing a large network of social media friends, feeling jealous of their lives and the fear of missing out on activities in online interactions.

Social anxiety can be defined as an excessive and persistent fear of what other people think of you, fear of being judged, criticised, or thought badly of by other people. Being afraid of doing something stupid, awkward, or embarrassing in front of others. Social anxiety is more than shyness, it is a fear that does not go away, and affects everyday activities, self-confidence, relationships and work or school life. Many people occasionally worry about social situations but a child or young person with social anxiety will show signs of feeling overly worried before, during and after them.

With the increase of mobile phones being accessible for even younger and younger people, real interactions have become a thing of the past. All you have to do is look down the road and you find at least one person who is glued to their phone. Research (Lee-Won, Herzog, Park, 2015) has shown that one of the main reasons why texting and other forms of social media are preferable, especially in the case of those struggling with social anxiety, to real-time interactions is that the awkward nature of conversation is replaced with a text, which can be edited and manipulated before it is sent, therefore allowing more control over the interaction than is possible in real-time social situations. However, even texting is being replaced by other apps such as the popular Snapchat, where pictures are sent instead of text.

When we look at social media, it can be a bit like Marmite, you either love it or you hate it. For some people, social media can be the perfect opportunity to pretend to be someone you are not. It is a way of hiding behind the real you and feeling under pressure to fit in with an image-obsessed culture. The BBC reported recently that children as young as five are suffering from insecurities about their weight, insecurities that are increasingly affecting boys as well as girls.

I have worked with children for over sixteen years and then went on to study a degree in psychology, so I have always been interested in how the mind and behaviour works. During my degree, I began to research how different media sources can have an impact on children's mental health and well-being. I began to notice more and more research that linked the two. There was an increase in young people complaining of mental health problems, such as body image and low self-confidence. It couldn't just be coincidence that more and more children and young people were suffering from mental health problems.

Teenagers are at a stage of life where peer-to-peer comparison increases in an effort to understand their identity. Self-identity in adolescence forms the basis of our self-esteem later on in life. Our children and young people are working to figure out who they are. Young people's identities are shaped by lots of factors: family, cultural and societal expectations, experiences within institutions such as school and the media, and most crucially friends. Young people are taking active steps and making choices that shape their identity. They select the environment and people they want to be around. They adjust their beliefs and behaviours based on feedback and they reflect on all of this whilst trying to figure out who they are.

With social media, it is easy to for them to lose their sense of identity and who they are by getting caught up in comparing themselves to other people. Instagram, for example, has a way of highlighting pressures for children and young people to grow up with unrealistic expectations and reinforce repeated messages that they are not enough just as they are.

For example, how many children or people do you know who are striving for "perfection". Seeing other prettier, more fashionable girls looking immaculate in a beautiful dress while they are travelling, which only makes them feel painfully conscious of the way that they don't always look that way. I bet if I asked, you would know someone who takes about twenty pictures before being happy with just one that they can post or send to someone.

What happened to the good old days where you could just take a lovely photo you were proud of and pop it up on Instagram to share with everyone?

I began to see how easy it is for social media to consume other people's lives; even I have been guilty of this myself. I started to recognise that I was checking my phone when I woke up, and it was the last thing I saw before I went to bed at night. I would be scrolling through my feed whenever I didn't know what else to do with myself. It was easy to just pick up my phone and watch a video or read lots of different posts.

I looked to Instagram for inspiration, but then I started worrying whether my pictures were good enough. I would spend hours editing my photos in order to get them to look exactly the way I wanted. I guess the thing with Instagram is we get so caught up in the online world that we begin to compare ourselves to other people's lives. It is so easy to look at someone else's picture who seems to be travelling the world, going out for meals on a daily basis and just "living their best life". It took a while for me to realise that this is the society we are living in. We are striving to be the best we can be but sometimes that means being someone who we think we want to be; it can be so easy to obsess over the way we look and not feel good enough as we are.

How many times do you find that you are comparing yourself to other girls or boys that you see on your thread? Do you find yourself wanting to dress like them? Do you start to worry that you are not good enough or beautiful or attractive like them?

Constantly checking for updates, statuses, comments and likes can generate massive amounts of worry and anxiety for a young person. The constant need to check up on what is happening on social media can cause sleep disturbances and can cause individuals to compare themselves to others.

Anxiety is a part of life, and everyone has feelings of anxiety at times, but it is important to stay connected with how you are feeling so you know when things are going wrong.

If there is one thing that I want to make you aware of is that social media makes you think, "Maybe I should be somewhere else, with someone else." If you always think your happiness is somewhere else, it will never be where you are. Sometimes, the universe has other plans for you and what you think you are missing out on can actually be a blessing in disguise.

If you realise that you are checking social media constantly, try taking the time to separate yourself from it. Social media can be fun but looking after your mental health is important. Self-care is key, and you must do what you can to protect yourself from being too invested in the virtual version of yourself. At the end of the day, it is more important to accept and love yourself for who you are in reality; loving that person is far more important than comparing yourself to virtual versions of people online.

Find something that you enjoy doing, such as a hobby or interest that you are really passionate about. Finding something else to focus on gave me something to look forward to when I got home from school or at the weekend. It made my day easier and, even if I felt incredibly uncomfortable, I knew that there was something good happening later.

Talking to someone about how you are feeling is really important – easier said than done, but don't be afraid to speak to a family member, or a friend you feel comfortable with. If you are not ready to speak to someone yet, then for some of my clients I ask them to write a letter to themselves explaining how they are feeling and why. I encourage them to be as open and truthful with themselves as they can be. After a few days, I then invite them to read it back to themselves, imagine that someone else wrote it and think about how they would help them. This has really helped some of them to think in a different way.

I want you to understand that how you are feeling is normal and that you are not alone. So many people around you have or are experiencing social anxiety. Just because you cannot see it doesn't mean it is not happening. I am writing this chapter because I know how it feels to constantly be worrying about what other people are thinking of you and changing who you are to try to fit in. It is one of the reasons I do the work that I do: I want every child and young person to feel seen, heard and validated. It has taken me years to become the woman I am today, but through the training and personal development work I have done, I learnt to overcome many of the challenges I faced and I know that you will too.

***

For every young person who is living with anxiety, I see you, hear you and validate you. Take this book as your permission to live life the way you want to, making good choices and setting boundaries. When you learn to love yourself from the inside out that is when true happiness begins.

Charlotte is a best-selling author, educator and consultant helping children and young people to find their voice, be seen and to feel validated. There is nothing she is more passionate about than making sure children know that they are loved and love themselves from the inside out. During her own childhood, Charlotte faced many struggles that only made her stronger. Through these experiences, she learnt that you can either sit down and cry about things or you get up and you move on, learning the lesson being shown to you.

After sixteen years' experience within different health and childcare settings, Charlotte gained a degree in psychology and is currently working towards a master's in children and young people.

Whilst working for the NHS, Charlotte realised just how precious life can be and that life can be cut short at any moment. So, charlotte decided to follow her passion and her love for children and young people to set up her own business, Mente Hermosa Academy (Beautiful Mind – Beautiful You in Spanish).

Charlotte has created her own CPD interactive training sessions that provide parents and childcare professionals with information on the current issues affecting children and young people, especially in regard to social media, body image and confidence issues.

Charlotte spends most of her time delivering training to nurseries, schools and organisations, offering workshops and retreats relating to emotional well-being.

Her mission is to provide support in order to bridge the gap with the mental health crisis that we are currently experiencing.

In between all this, you will often find Charlotte travelling the world and making the most out of life.

https://linktr.ee/mentehermosaacademy

Listen to the audio version here:
https://bit.ly/Socialmediaandanxiety

NAVIGATING YOUR WAY THROUGH ANXIETY

A Teen's Exam Anxiety Survival Guide –
Proven Tips to Overcome Fear, Panic and Worry

Clare Ford

*"The day came when the risk to remain in a bud was
more painful than the risk it took to blossom."*
– Anais Nin

"Children are not defined by their grades."
– Clare Ford

So why is this the new age of anxiety for teenagers?

Our narrow definition of success as parents, teachers and society at large is a significant contributor to teenage anxiety. Acceptable outcomes are, for the most part, purely objective: "You need to achieve this grade to get into this college, make this team, play in this orchestra…"

Our own anxiety often has us pressing an agenda on children from a very early age. I am constantly amazed at how over-scheduled and over-stimulated children I tutor are – how very little space they have to just simply relax and be a child. In fact, one of the positives from the pandemic was that families had to stop tearing around from pillar to post, from clubs and groups and classes, and stay at home to learn, rest and play. And that was SO HARD!

The problem is that this linear pathway to achievement, and the benchmarks that are measured along the road to success, does not allow for individuality. It folds our kids and teens into very small, constricted boxes with very little space for play, self-expression, experimentation or thriving. It does nothing for the self-esteem of the teen who is creative, artistic or whacky.

By restricting our children and teens into these small, unimaginative boxes, we are creating two significant problems that create high degrees of anxiety in teens, especially when they think about their future.

Firstly, their natural gifts, talents, interests and attributes are often completely overlooked – they are forced into classes or fields in which they have no particular interest or acumen because it's "expected" or the "done thing". Unsurprisingly, allowing your teen to follow her interest and encouraging her to do so is exactly what will bring her "success". Fitting her neatly onto an acceptable resumé will result in feelings of hopelessness, despair and failure. How do I know? I coach teens with this on a weekly basis.

Because of the narrow definition of success that we are imposing on young people, I have seen first-hand how discouraged they are. Instead, we have to guide them towards their light, not some false, tired narrative designed to satisfy other people's definitions of success.

Without creative, outside-the-box innovators, artists and inventors, the human race will simply stagnate! Curiosity, critical thinking and collaboration are key skills that industries are looking for in their future employees – not robots who can rote learn and memorise facts.

Howard Gardner[1] proposes that there are eight innate intelligences (spatial, bodily-kinesthetic, musical, interpersonal, intrapersonal, naturalistic, linguistic and logical-mathematical), and yet children leave school being measured (and therefore defined to a large extent) on just two of them: verbal/linguistic and logical-mathematical.

Below I suggest some things that we can do as parents and educators to really allow our children to be seen in their true essence, for whom they really are, and for the wonderful uniqueness they bring to enrich our world.

In fact, research and experience suggest that raising happy, healthy, flourishing kids requires parents to do just one key thing. It's not about reading all the parenting best sellers or signing your kids up for all the right activities. You don't even have to know exactly what you're doing. Just show up and CONNECT. Showing up means bringing your whole being – your attention and awareness – into this moment with your child. When we show up, we are mentally and emotionally present for our child right now.

Longitudinal research[2] on child and teen development suggests that one of the best predictors for how any child turns out – in terms of happiness, social and emotional development, meaningful relationships, and even academic and career success – is having received sensitive, supportive care early in life.

Seeing our teens also means being willing to look beyond our initial assumptions and interpretations. If your teen is quiet when she meets someone new, you might assume she is being impolite and try to improve her social skills. But she may simply be feeling shy or anxious. Rather than immediately correcting manners, you should first observe where she is right now, and work to understand the feelings behind the behaviour. Even in our most well-meaning moments, we can fall into the trap of hoping our kids will be something other than who they really are. We might want a teen to be studious or athletic or artistic or neat or achievement-orientated or something else. But what if he just doesn't care about kicking a ball into a net? Or is even unable to do so? What if she has no interest in playing the flute? What if it doesn't seem important to get straight A's, or it feels inauthentic to conform to gender norms?

You probably know the dad who pushes his disinterested son onto the football pitch, or the mum who insists her introverted child go to a drama class, regardless of the child's inclinations. These parents are failing to see who their children really are.

That sets up a despairing reality: there are some young adults who have lived a majority of their childhoods not being seen and trying to "please" the adults around them. Never feeling understood. Rarely having the experience that someone feels their feelings, takes on their perspective, knows their likes and dislikes. Imagine how these children feel – invisible and alone. When they think about their teachers, their peers, even their parents, one thought can run through their minds: "They don't get me at all."

Pressing children through middle school and high school, loading them up with extra-curricular activities and hours and hours of homework to push through a rigorous school curriculum towards the highest possible level of achievement is simply setting them up for disaster.

The point is to develop an attitude of curiosity rather than immediate judgment.

Let us courageously and boldly teach a more balanced approach and encourage teens to foster an individualised definition of success. Finding schools, colleges and universities that are a "good fit" and accepting that getting less than nine A*s is absolutely okay will do more to boost confidence and lessen anxiety for our teens – although it may heighten those of the adults around them as we have to adjust giving up some vision of our dreams for them. It requires a dramatic show of faith that your teen is capable of discovering his path on his own if we give him the space to do so.

Through this process, young people build confidence, build resilience, build resourcefulness and build their self-esteem. They work hard and "show up" for themselves. They become intrinsically motivated and will do what it takes to move towards their goals. How do I know? Because I mentor teens to Discover Their Path.

I offer below some practical advice for parents and teens that I have shared with many families over the years to help them prepare for stressful situations, such as taking exams, tests or interviews, and they have reported back that these strategies have been very useful. I hope you can use them at home or at school too! Let me know how you get on.

1) Make a REALISTIC revision timetable

"If you fail to plan you are planning to fail"
– Benjamin Franklin

In our Acing Your Exams clinics, we talk about timetabling revision from the get-go, but prioritising regular rest breaks, treats and time to meet up with friends or go on social media. We also bear in mind a teen's natural biorhythms and sleeping patterns so that the majority of revision is done after lunch! It's important to plan out the whole revision period including during the exams to take into consideration how long to keep momentum going.

Tochi, aged twelve, says:

"I have learnt that timetables can be useful when you are learning your weak subjects and so when that day comes, you don't have to be that overwhelmed to take the exam."

2) Practise, practise, practise!

Use past papers to apply revision notes and concepts and practise writing out and timing questions. Many young adults find it difficult to write for long periods of time, simply because we type and text and rarely jot down much on paper.

Kelechi, Amarachi and Deja, aged thirteen to fourteen, say:

"Keep timings accurate"

"Making sure I calculate times"

"Don't stick to one question for a long period of time"

3) Stay physically healthy using the SHED Method[3] by Sarah Milne Rowe

S – Sleep – less screentime in the evening just before bed.
H – Hydration – increase water intake daily.
E – Exercise – regularly, and outside in nature if possible.
D – Diet – balanced diet, cut out sugar, fast food and caffeine.

Esha, aged fifteen, said in our SMART goal setting session:

"I will improve...
Exercise – I lost my interest in sport; 20 min walk daily!
Diet – could be improved; replace junk food with mangoes
Hydration – I definitely need to be drinking more water"

4) Manage brain freeze during the exams using the B.U.I.L.D Method, created by me!

B – Breathwork – using three rounds of "rectangular" breathing to calm the parasympathetic nervous system and reduce the levels of cortisol, adrenalin and noradrenalin in the body and brain.

U – Unwind – stretch arms up and gently stretch the neck to release tension and trapped, stagnant energy.

I – Imagine – close your eyes for a couple of seconds and see yourself answering the questions and finishing the paper with ease.

L – Listen – to the critical inner voice telling you that you can't do it. Acknowledge the message, decide that it's unhelpful and simply thank your inner self for trying to keep you safe, but that you can do it and that nothing bad will happen.

D – Do – just start jotting down some ideas and have a go at an easier question to build momentum.

5) Understand that test anxiety is perfectly normal and a healthy response

The key is to manage the stress well and to maximise your performance in the exam. We know you are resilient, and we are confident that you can manage everything that is expected of you.

6) Get support – you don't have to do this alone

Find a group of friends, a parent or relative or trusted adult who is happy to simply listen without judgement.

I would love to know what you have found useful!

NOTES

[1] In his book, *Multiple Intelligences*, Gardner defines an intelligence as "bio-psychological potential to process information that can be activated in a cultural setting to solve problems or create products that are of value in a culture."[58] According to Gardner, there are more ways to do this than just through logical and linguistic intelligence. Gardner believes that the purpose of schooling "should be to develop intelligences and to help people reach vocational and avocational goals that are appropriate to their particular spectrum of intelligences. People who are helped to do so, [he] believe[s], feel more engaged and competent and therefore more inclined to serve society in a constructive way."[a]

Gardner contends that IQ tests focus mostly on logical and linguistic intelligence. Upon doing well on these tests, the chances of attending a prestigious college or university increase, which in turn creates contributing members of society.[59] While many students function well in this environment, there are those who do not. Gardner's theory argues that students will be better served by a broader vision of education, wherein teachers use different methodologies, exercises and activities to reach all students, not just those who excel at linguistic and logical intelligence. It challenges educators to find "ways that will work for this student learning this topic".[60]

[2] This longitudinal study investigated the process whereby early parent involvement in preschool affects student achievement from kindergarten through to sixth grade. Early parent involvement directly influenced kindergarten achievement, which in turn influenced first grade student motivation. Highly motivated children then encouraged parents to continue involvement. Findings suggest that early parent involvement sets the stage for subsequent parent involvement, student motivation, and academic achievement throughout early and middle childhood.

[3] *The SHED Method* (published in Jan 2018) introduces the mind management framework that Coaching Impact founder Sara Milne Rowe uses to help clients make better energy choices and be their best, when it matters most. Sarah Milne Rowe is one of the UK's leading performance coaches, working with CEOs, senior leaders and teams, often in high challenge situations, so they can stay strong, keep learning and deliver their best.

★★★

I dedicate this to my two sons, Alex and Oskar.

Clare is an award-winning international author, speaker, coach, healer, educator and parent who is passionate about ensuring that children and teens are "switched on" learners, accessing their natural gifts, abilities and talents to discover their true potential and live purposefully.

Founder of Switched ON!, the global online academy, and an academic coach with over twenty years' experience, Clare combines her unique skill set using her SWITCHED ON! learning method to unlock the brilliance in your child, tween or teen.

Please connect with me further here:
linktr.ee/switchedonacademy1

Listen to the audio version here:
https://bit.ly/teenexamanxietysurvivalguide

PERFORMANCE ANXIETY

Charlotte West

"Sing like no one is listening."
— *Mark Twain*

Do you love performing? Surely, if you're a singer or musician, you must love performing. Do you get nervous? How many times have I heard that? I can't even count on one hand, probably not even on ten hands!

You may be thinking, 'I want to perform. I love performing and that's my job.' You're motivated by your audience and the fact that you want to make a positive impact on people's lives. But then you step out onto that stage and everything changes in an instant. Every time you try to perform for an audience, this wave of anxiety washes over you and you go into panic. Does this sound familiar? Well, if it does, then what you are experiencing is what is also known as stage fright. So, in its simplest terms, performance anxiety is stage fright.

The fear of performing before and/or during a performance, anxiety can come in all different shapes and sizes. Some people will be nervous beforehand, walk out on stage and it will disappear, and for others it may not, it may continue for the whole performance. In most cases, the reason is the fear of failure, that you've not prepared enough. The feeling that you're not good enough, that the audience aren't going to like you. Does this sound familiar?

It doesn't matter whether you are a singer, musician, actor, dancer, public speaker, etc. You may still get performance anxiety; lots of performers get it, it's not just you. It is completely normal to experience this and natural to experience a little bit of nervousness before you go on to stage to perform. For some, this nervousness (which is, in fact, a surge of adrenaline) increases the performance focus and intensity on stage, but for others, performance anxiety can be debilitating to the point that they can even pass out or have panic attacks right there on stage. It can have an impact on their ability to perform and, in the worst case scenario, for some, end their performance career.

There can be lots of things at play when a person is suffering from performance anxiety, just like other forms of anxiety. Here are some examples: the location of the performance, whether you already suffer from anxiety, who is coming to the performance, your vocal ability or prior preparation. The list is endless. However, for the purpose of this chapter, we are going to focus on the voice itself, vocal health and a few strategies that you may want to consider.

This may seem like a question with an obvious answer, but if you went to the gym, would you warm up? If you did any kind of sport would you warm up? If the answer is yes, then you will know exactly what I mean when I say that warming up is essential to protect your muscles! Warming up is an essential part of good vocal health too. If you don't warm up a muscle, how do you expect it to work efficiently?

Your vocal muscles are just like in any other sport or physical activity. There are some days when your voice may need a longer warm up than others, depending on how much you've used it, what you've eaten and drunk, how hydrated you are and also your hormones (something that is becoming more vocalised).

One of the most beneficial exercises for warming up your voice is something we call a 'semi occluded vocal tract' exercise (SOVT for short), which in the simplest terms means that your mouth is partially closed, so there is an increased back pressure, which reflects at the lips back to the vocal folds to help them vibrate with more ease and less effort. In my language, it allows the muscles to 'kiss' and discourages unwanted tension, giving a chance for the muscles to work effectively and freely.

Within this chapter, I will give examples of SOVT exercises to help you along the way. There are many other exercises that you can do to warm up your voice and, in most parts, they are tailored to the individual, just like you would tailor other things in life for the individual. So, if you want the right exercises for YOUR voice, get advice from a qualified vocal coach.

When singing or performing, you need to know your limits of how long you need to warm up per day. Now, this can depend on your age, and also how long you've been singing. So, whether you think fifteen minutes, half an hour, forty-five minutes or an hour a day is suitable, the best people to ask are professionals. If you have proper vocal training, you will build up stamina just like you do in sport, and that stamina will allow you to progress. Each time you sing, you will be able to increase that stamina. However, it is important not to overwork it.

Just like any other muscle, if you overwork it, the muscle gets tired. This is where I talk about vocal damage and vocal injury. I won't go into the extent of these, however just be aware that vocal damage can be quite serious and if you think you may have encountered vocal damage, however young or old you are, please visit a professional. This may include an ear, nose and throat doctor (ENT), speech and language therapist (SLT) and a vocal coach that specialises in vocal rehabilitation (the next part of my journey). I know it's scary but visiting that professional will save your voice. In simple terms, it is someone to heal you and someone to work through that healing. Vocal damage can be very serious and can lead to many complications, including ending your singing career, so please (and I say this with love) do take it seriously.

In a session, as part of vocal health, when I first meet a student, I do a diagnostic analysis, almost like a prescription. I discuss things like a student's age, how long they've been singing, whether they have got any singing experience, how much they sing and whether they are on any medications.

Medications obviously vary from person to person and have different effects. Some medications can cause side effects that will affect singing. I am not saying not to take that medication, or change the medication at all, as I am not medically trained. However, as a vocal coach/singing teacher I need to be aware of that medication to ensure your safety. I appreciate that in some cases it may feel a little bit vulnerable for some children and young people, but singing teachers are friendly. We are here to listen and if you are taking any medication that you think may affect your singing, then please do disclose it to your teacher or coach.

Another major part of vocal health is WATER. Water is your friend; to have a healthy voice, your vocal folds need to be hydrated. Sip water throughout your day. Make sure you take water to a performance. Water acts as a sprinkler, it glides over the top of your vocal folds and keeps them moist. Hydrated vocal folds = a happy voice.

You might be thinking, what on earth is she going on about? How does she know about all this? There are two straightforward answers to this: one being that I have trained extensively looking at vocal health, performance anxiety and vocal pedagogy. The other one is that I was that young adult performing with performance anxiety and vocal health issues. This is why I want to educate other young people in this area. The more open performers are about these concerns, the more of the norm they become and the less pressure it creates on young people today.

So now for the link between vocal health and performance anxiety? I will give you a little snippet of what can potentially happen: you grow up singing, all your life you've been singing, it's what you want to do, you have done it from a very young age and you don't know any different. You've had many singing teachers along the way, who have given you different advice. You go on to do GCSE, A level, undergraduate degree and postgraduate degrees. You also already have performance anxiety to a certain degree. You already get nervous when singing. It's the fear of being vulnerable in front of someone, baring your emotion and fear of failure.

But as your singing career progresses, and your singing journey starts to take flight, you over practice and you don't drink enough water. You spend long, late hours in the rehearsal room. You don't warm up (because your teacher tells you it's not necessary). You have to be the best. You find your happy place and you just keep going and going. You use that muscle over and over again. You try to keep quiet on occasions, but university life doesn't allow you to do that because you're always out dancing, drinking and having fun with your friends. Until one day when you finish your degree you are in a masterclass. You stand up, go to sing and nothing! Your performance anxiety triples, your fear of failure goes through the roof and you have no voice.

No one can advise you what to do. You are scared and you go to professional after professional. The thing you've always wanted to do is singing and now that joy of singing has been taken away from you. Performance anxiety gradually increases because you are relying on an instrument that is no longer reliable. You've failed! You try to stand on stage, but still nothing comes out. You feel sweaty, you feel scared, your arms and your legs start to shake. Your voice starts to shake uncontrollably so that you have no chance of singing and, finally, you find yourself in the middle of the stage in a heap on the floor, feeling nauseous and having just passed out.

I'm not saying any of this to scare you, more so to educate you and let you know what can be done to help and how to deal with it. I was not educated. I did not go and see a professional like an ENT. I visited a vocal coach in London who advised me to be quiet for six months. It was terrifying. Now can you see the link between vocal health and performance anxiety?

After years and years of having performance anxiety, I decided enough was enough. I took the bull by the horns and decided to study vocal pedagogy. This is the study of the art and science of the voice, looking at the anatomy, how it is used within teaching and how to accomplish singing technique. I decided that I wanted to educate young people and children about performance anxiety, vocal health and give them good singing coaching that they could use for the rest of their lives. Skills they could use in whatever path they take.

I am still a work in progress, like we always are, but now I am educated, I need to get out there and sing myself, which, again, is still a work in progress. I decided that I wanted to crack this performance anxiety and lead the life that I was meant to lead. I wanted to take it that step further and look at how the mind works and how this also has an impact on performance anxiety. So, I took sessions with a professional in performance anxiety, a gentleman called David Juncos who uses acceptance and commitment therapy (ACT). Then I discovered the wonderful world of neuro linguistic programming, or NLP for short.

NLP is full of wonderful tools and techniques to help you manage your day-to-day life and deal with the fears and worries that you have. I admit I was a little sceptical of the holistic approach, and in the past had listened to the advice of SO many professionals that I'd almost become despondent. But I can honestly say that NLP has changed my life.

What is NLP? NLP is looking at neuroscience, the language and our programming. In NLP, we look at the physical component as well as the mental and emotional components of neurology. It looks at linguistics of the language that we use and how we communicate with others, and how we also communicate with ourselves. The programming itself is how we internalise it and the way our past experiences and thoughts and emotions affect all areas of our lives, the language in which we speak to ourselves and internalise it. The user manual for the brain.

The reason I decided to use NLP within my training is because how we talk to our mind and ourselves, and how we interpret our experiences, past and present affects the way in which we sing. It also affects not only the way we sing, but how we react to singing.

Our aim in NLP is to work with our conscious mind to speak to our unconscious mind kindly and with forgiveness to allow it the chance to tell us what we really want in life.

When looking at performance anxiety and looking at experiences that we have been through during the anxiety, our mind likes to fight and try to control the experience and our conscious mind almost gets in the way. Therefore, with the use of NLP, you are able to speak to your unconscious mind in a safe way and get to the root of the desire or desired outcome, therefore freeing you and allowing you to express yourself in a safe environment. When we speak to our unconscious mind, it tells us the answers and we are able to use that to guide us to a less stressful experience.

For example, if you were going on stage and, every time you go onto stage, you get anxiety and your hands begin to shake, your legs begin to shake and then your voice begins to shake uncontrollably and you have no control whatsoever over your performance, this is a state that has been built into you because of anxiety. It is like a cycle, a learned behaviour that we repeat. If NLP is used prior to a performance to create a state of mind that is more free and more relaxed and used as a prevention, it can create a more enjoyable experience, allowing the mind to feel less anxious and your symptoms to be reduced, even gone.

Reflecting on all of the above, you can see that there is a correlation between vocal health and performance anxiety, using NLP as a further intervention. Ensuring that you have good vocal health can reduce performance anxiety and early intervention is key. This is not the only cause of performance anxiety, but it can be a contributing factor.

In the audio provided, please find some SOVT

exercises, a meditation and some exercises for you to try: Finding your Voice Meditation: https://bit.ly/findingyourvoicemeditation and SOVT exercises: https://bit.ly/sovtexercises

Be kind to yourself; remember that you are safe, performance anxiety is normal, talk to others and there are professionals to help. You are not alone.

★★★

For my wonderful mum and dad.
Without you, none of this would have been possible. Thank you for all your love and support. You are my inspiration!
Love you xxx

Stylistically diverse, Charlotte's singing career has seen her perform as a soloist with the world-renowned BBC Philharmonic Orchestra at the Royal Albert Hall and, in 2012, at the Paralympic Games Torch Ceremony alongside Tinie Tempah, as well as at a host of other venues and events.

Originally training as a classical singer, Charlotte graduated with a BA(Hons) in music performance in 2007. Following on from this, she gained an MA in community music in 2008.

After overcoming issues related to voice loss and performance anxiety, Charlotte found a desire to pass on the knowledge she had gained from her experiences. This led her to complete a post graduate certificate professional voice practice exploring the diversity of the voice, thereby giving her coaching the flexibility to meet the demands of her clients – children and adults alike.

Charlotte is always learning and considers herself to be a work in progress along with her performance anxiety. With this, she decided to become a practitioner in neuro linguistic programming that made a dramatic difference in her journey.

Charlotte's ethos is to empower young people and adults to have a voice that is heard, a voice that is nurtured and for people to love singing as much as she does and to have fun!

https://linktr.ee/charlottewest

Listen to the audio version here:
https://bit.ly/performanceanxietyCW

YOUR JOURNEY, YOUR CHOICE

Ashleigh Quick

A diagnosis of cancer or other life limiting illness can be difficult to cope with. Not only do we have to deal with our own anxieties, but those anxieties others feel; for example, by our children. It's completely normal to feel frightened, anxious and unsure where the road ahead will take us, but remember this: you are not alone. It's not easy to decide what or when to tell our children something so painful, that you have cancer, or that you have a life limiting disease.

Through my many years as a chemotherapy nurse practitioner, I have worked closely with families and friends to be part of their journey. It has been an honour; it's one of the most rewarding things I have accomplished in my life. Telling an adult loved one you have a terminal illness can be overwhelming, and many find this the hardest part of their journey, especially when that diagnosis is terminal. Telling a child brings its own difficulties, but these can be made easier.

Firstly, you should think about you: how do *you* feel? Secondly, think about what you are comfortable to share with others. You may ask yourself, "How will I say those words?" You yourself may be struggling to cope with the diagnosis and prognosis, therefore you need to be ready to answer questions from your child should they arise. And they will – sometimes over a bowl of cornflakes or skipping on the way to school – but, more often, they arise at night during your bedtime routine. Children feel safe when being tucked in at night, and feel more comfortable to ask you questions, to talk about what's on their mind. There are many support networks in the world to help guide and support you through your cancer journey.

There is no right way to tell a loved one or child you have a terminal illness; what is right for one family, may not be right for you. You must be comfortable and at ease with the decision you are making and how you want to go about it. Remember, this is your illness and your child/children. Some parents tell their children as soon as they are diagnosed and some wait until they have more information regarding their treatment plan.

When talking about cancer, we need to be open and honest, and there are many benefits to this. Children are far more able to notice change, pick up on things; they know when something is not right. Their intuition is their superpower. Older children may begin to research things themselves, which can increase their anxiety about what's really happening. When we stop talking to our children, they can begin to worry more, and the sums begin to add up incorrectly. Their imaginations are their magic, but this can also lead to anxieties. They may fill the gaps with fears, and this can be worse than them knowing the truth. They also have big ears, they may overhear a conversation, and find out another way; this can break down the trust between you and your child.

All we want to do as a parent is protect our children. We worry that they worry, or that they won't cope with certain situations. But if they did know, could this perhaps lead them to a sense of feeling in control? As already mentioned, they have amazing intuition. Speaking openly gives them an opportunity to ask questions.

Many parents choose a special place, somewhere they know their child feels safe and comfortable. Maybe not in a public place, so they and you feel more comfortable to show emotions. Although many questions arise from children at night, it's thought that telling your child your diagnosis at night can cause them not to sleep, so talk to them in the day so they can process that information before bed and ask any burning questions they may have.

If you have children of different ages, you may want to tell them separately and in a different way. You can always bring everyone together after. Or you can tell them together. Remember, this is your journey, your family.

Understanding your children is key here. It's very difficult to find the right words. Being optimistic can lead to false hope, but it can be hard to tell them the truth. All children will want to know something different. The most common question is, "Does it hurt?" because it's exactly what we say when they have bumped their knee or have a tummy ache. What they really want to hear is that you still love them and always will, no matter what happens.

If your child is older, sometimes we can ask them if

they have noticed anything different at home lately. They may surprise you with what they already know.

Be clear and concise if you can. Use simple words. You will still be getting your own head around medical terminology. Break it down, tell them a little at a time if you feel this is right for them, build on the information you tell them in order to not overwhelm them and yourself. Some parents ask their children how much they want to know. I have come across patients who want to know everything, they write notes, undertake research to better understand their diagnosis, but there are also people who just want to know what they need to, the minimum amount of information is best for them. It's no different for your child.

Many parents have said they were surprised at how their child reacted. That they just shrugged it off. Please don't worry about this, they will all react differently. Questions, children love questions, and its okay to say, "I don't know." You're not expected to have all the answers, but it's good to know they have listened and taken on board what you have said. Talking to your child means we have a better understanding of what they may have misunderstood, for us to best support and reassure them.

Very young children will not be able to understand about your illness, but they will still at any age be able to pick up on your feelings, on changes in your physical appearance. Primary age children will have possibly heard the word cancer but will not be able to understand a condition that isn't really spoken about – a rare disease, for example. Their understanding will be basic. They often tend to think you are unwell because they have done something wrong or that they may catch it like they may catch chickenpox. As our children grow, they begin to have a better understanding of cancer, the effects of illness and how our bodies work and sometimes don't work. Here they are just beginning to understand that people can be very unwell.

Teenagers might understand a little more – maybe more of the biology of cells and our bodies – but remember here that they can still have misconceptions and often believe things that are untrue. Just talk to them. This is where you as a parent can find out if they have misunderstood anything; this is your opportunity to correct those misunderstandings.

Most parents fear and become anxious about how their child will react. This will generally depend on your relationship with them, their ability to understand, how mature they are, their age, their emotional maturity or how they control or express their emotions. Remember, all children need the same love and reassurance; maybe that's reassurance that it's not their fault, as children often feel they are to blame.

It's important to really tune in to your child. Younger children will not be able to express themselves with words as an older child might. Younger, primary school aged children will express themselves through play. They may play games such as making dens, where they can hide but feel secure. Or maybe through their mood; they may become unsettled, withdrawn, become naughty, they may start to show off, be disruptive. Your child may become clingy, or unsettled at bedtime. They may start sucking their thumb. New fears can arise for them too, such as having the lights out at night, and bed wetting. Some may have no reaction at all, and this is fine. These are just some of the ways your child can express their feelings.

For older children, and teenagers especially, this is an already difficult time for them. They are at the age when they are finding their place in the world, who they are, how they are seen by others; it's an emotional roller coaster. Although older children and teenagers are better able to express themselves through words, remember they too can have similar behaviour changes too. They need time to process, to grieve the news. They may also not be so forthcoming with questions, so it's important here to let them have one-to-one time so they feel safe to express to you how they are feeling. Guilt is very common. They are just beginning to find their feet, their place in the world, becoming independent, but with a parent who is unwell they may want to be at home with you as they may not want you to be alone. Ensure you make it clear that you are there for them, that they can ask you categorically anything at all.

Teenagers will often plod on, finding it difficult to ask for support. This is where schools, counsellors, family and friends may need to step in. This is not a failure on your part, it's just life, and it's okay to ask for help. Teenagers often find it easier to talk to friends or someone from your school support network. They won't want to add to your stress and worry, and may not want you to see them upset. So, a safe space is essential to support your teenager or older child. I feel it's important here to reiterate that their behaviour could possibly change dramatically; mood swings, depression, self-harm. Support in the teenage years is essential. You need to look out for physical signs that they are not coping, such as headaches, stomach pains and eating changes.

It's your choice, your decision, and they are your children. There is no right time or right way to talk about something so painful. But we do need to bear in mind that secrets can be stressful. When the time feels right for you, try and be prepared. Saying the words "I have cancer" are hard enough; try saying them out loud to yourself beforehand, as they are understandably hard words to hear, but to say them can be difficult too. You could find some resources – such as books for younger children – there is so much out there to support you.

It may not go as planned and this is fine; no one knows – not even you – how your child/children will react. One of the hardest questions you may hear from your child is, "Are you going to die?" Thinking about how you answer this question beforehand can reduce your anxieties and stress. It's important not to dismiss this question, as hard as it may be to answer. Most children will have this question but may not verbally express it.

I'm going to finish by listing some activities and practical ways to support your child:

- Routine is essential here, don't alter it unless absolutely necessary.
- Have fun, family time and one-to-one time with each child.
- A worry box is a great way for your child to write down how they feel. It may be empty for a while but be patient.
- Listen to your child, watch them, and remember younger children express themselves through play.
- Find different ways to communicate things – a family diary, a wall chart, etc. – so they know what's happening on what day. Include them in family decisions, no matter what their age.
- Reach out, ask for help, inform the school, college and other support networks you have.
- Most importantly, just love them and be there for them. This is your life, your children and there is no right way or wrong way. It's your journey.

I will end now with a quote by Pooh bear:

> "If ever there is a tomorrow when we're not together, there is something you must always remember: you are braver than you believe, stronger than you seem, and smarter than you think, but the most important thing is even when we're apart... I'll always be with you."

★★★

In dedication to my wonderful mum Patricia Quick and my dad John Leslie Quick. Mum, you have always supported me through my life personally and academically. You always had faith and offered encouragement to succeed in every aspect of my life. Your support and words of encouragement enabled me to be cope as a single parent and follow my dream to become a chemotherapy nurse practitioner, a dream I had since my father passed away from leukaemia when I was nine. Mum, I love you and thank you, and Daddy, I hope you're proud of the person I am today; your departure from this world enabled me to offer support to many cancer patients and their families.

Ashleigh Quick is a mother of two beautiful children, a boy and a girl now aged eighteen and twenty, and is extremely proud of them both. Ashleigh qualified as a nurse in 1996, and then went on to study a degree and master's in oncology and palliative care. She has worked as a chemotherapy nurse specialist for over twenty-six years. During her spare time, she enjoys carp fishing, yoga, walking, reading and spending quiet time with her family. Ashleigh has always seen herself as an empath and strives to put others first. She thrives on learning new things and qualified as an NLP practitioner in 2020 and a hypnosis practitioner in 2022.

Ashleigh has always been passionate about helping others. She has a free Facebook group where she offers a different yet powerful approach to managing chronic pain and unwanted chemotherapy side effects. Ashleigh herself has been a chronic pain sufferer for many years and was shown the power of NLP and hypnosis to relieve symptoms. This led to her forming her own path to help others as she has been helped. She also assists families with the difficult task of talking to their children regarding life limiting conditions and the potential outcome.

https://linktr.ee/ashleigh_hp

Listen to the audio version here:
https://bit.ly/yourjourneyyourchoice

AUTISM AND ANXIETY DOES NOT DEFINE ME

Emily Nuttall

*"I think every person has their own identity and beauty.
Everyone being different is what is really beautiful. If we
were all the same, it would be boring."*
— *Tila Tequila*

Becoming a parent is one of the most amazing things in the world. To know that you created a child so special and unique, you anticipate that you will go on this smooth journey like a car speeding down the straight road, with no bumps, no diversions, crossroads, or emergency stops, reaching your final destination believing that you developed and nurtured your child to be able to thrive, succeed, be the best that they can be and in the hope they go on to become a parent to an incredible child of their own one day.

When your child is born, at the very beginning they create this attachment to you, like a lamb snuggling close into its mum's soft white coat where it feels safe, protected and warm, unaware of what is ahead of them. They go through an incredible journey of physical, intellectual, emotional, spiritual and social growth and development to become the amazing, unique children that they are. You hope that everything will be smooth and plain sailing and that there will never be any worries, struggles, challenges or concerns, just like when we watch and read all kinds of magical fairy-tales. But, as we know, sadly, life isn't as simple as that.

The reason you have probably felt the need to pick up this book and feel drawn to reading my chapter is that you have found yourself in the middle of your journey having hit some crossroads with the challenges you are facing, as you try to understand the challenges of autism and anxiety linked together.

Having been that child, teenager and now young adult still with these experiences and the other challenges that have come alongside it, since then it has been like looking in a mirror of a past reflection of myself and watching the journey my mother and family had to navigate at that time, which was like a train going through a dark, long tunnel filled with so much uncertainty, unknowns, worry, confusion and fear, but also full of light, hope, support, encouragement and care. They would have found this book helpful to equip them with the understanding, tools and resources to be able to make sense of and process my feelings, challenges and struggles as I went through life with this experience of autism and anxiety together hand in hand, but also realise the unique, resilient Emily it has made me today.

What I am about to share with you I hope will equip you, empower you, inspire you, and help to create long-lasting change for the better, showing you that I am proof that autism and anxiety do not have to define your child's life but can actually be a superpower to help your child and you as a family achieve whatever you want and allow you to be proud of the amazing children that they are and be able to commend yourself as parents for doing your very best.

Autism and anxiety, what does this actually mean? What does it look like? What happens? What helps? My own definition of autism from my own experience, research and understanding, as I have learnt about my diagnosis over the years, is that autism is defined as a neurological development condition. It can also be classed as being on an autism spectrum, which is the phrase for determining the degree of how that person's autism has an impact on them. But each experience is individual, different and unique for each person in terms of how it has an impact on their everyday lives and their daily routines, relationships, behaviour, communication, interaction, imagination, connection with the world, background noises, unexpected plan changes, unpredictable life challenges, and sensory overload. When you throw anxiety into the mix with this it can be referred to as your "overwhelm bucket" that is full and overflowing and, if the bucket becomes full, your child will experience what is described as a "meltdown".

Meltdowns (not the everyday tantrums that you instantly think about when a child is unable to get their own way) are best described as an extreme response to any life situation that may overwhelm your child and make them feel fearful and out of control. This could include going to school, attending medical appointments, outside hobbies and activities, crowded, noisy or new environments. The way that a meltdown would present could include verbal expressions such as shouting, screaming, crying, physical reactions such as punching, biting, kicking, hitting and sometimes one or both of these can present at any time. When a child experiences this, they are unable to understand and make sense of what is happening in their minds, almost like a churning washing machine going at full spin. Sometimes, though, it is also important to be aware that meltdowns can be where a child may shut down and not interact at all; they may completely withdraw from these situations, as it helps to prevent them from becoming overwhelmed and anxious.

When meltdowns happen, it is important to not be angry or judge that child experiencing it as it isn't their fault. It is important to identify the causes of your child's meltdown once they have happened, reduce the triggers, think of the sensory situations in that environment and be creative and expressive with change and routine to help your child understand what is happening, therefore allowing you to put effective, creative plans and strategies in place to help. This link will explain more: https://www. autism.org.uk/advice-and-guidance/topics/behaviour/ meltdowns/all-audiences

How did autism, anxiety and meltdowns feel for me? My best analogy for this was like a two-litre fizzy drink bottle that has been shaken constantly, building pressure and not having that pressure released, therefore exploding.

All my emotions, thoughts, feelings, the triggers for these were all fizzed up and mixed together. I was confused, lost and scared. I couldn't make sense of what was happening or how to express what I was thinking and feeling, which would result in me experiencing violent outbursts, including me screaming, lashing out, having panic attacks and smashing everything up around me like a bomb exploding. I was scared, lost and alone, trapped in my own little isolated bubble, unable to know where I belonged in the world around me.

What were my darkest moments and challenges in these experiences? Sometimes children like myself, when they are overwhelmed and consumed by their overwhelm bucket, their lives, emotions, social pressures, thoughts and feelings and anxiety can lead to very difficult coping strategies. This was where I started to experience my struggles with self-harm, through punching, cutting, pulling my hair and anorexia, as ways of trying to navigate, process and manage my anxieties, emotions and feelings, release my anger and frustrations and shut down to feel safe and not hurt anyone around me. I also experienced severe panic attacks and I can describe that as like my chest being crushed and my heart beating at 100 miles an hour, almost like my brain was waiting to explode outside of my mind. I was often running away and all of this left me feeling so alone, lost, confused and scared. This whole ordeal left me needing to be safely restrained to be able to keep me safe. In my head, it made me feel like I was a criminal, but I realise now it was to protect and hold me, eventually calming me, followed by hugs from Mum and teddy bears to soothe me afterwards, making it all feel better.

Being able to find and ensure that I could have a safe place in every environment that I was in was so important, as needing to feel grounded, safe and in a place where I could be calm, even just by a wall with different colours or shapes, holding fidget toys or my favourite bear, would be a comfort, a release and enable me to be almost going on my own little story adventure, feeling free. Being able to draw and write and have those options with me to express myself in any environment was also crucial to this. Having meal plans with safe foods and having food exposure, creative and talking therapy helped my anxieties around feeling safe with food again, processing my emotions and supporting my ongoing recovery.

A huge positive and turning point in this journey was being referred to the family intervention and family services. My mum and I were given the support of family support workers, social workers, support and social groups, the CAMHS mental health and eating disorder team with specialist professionals like an army of support soldiers marching by our sides giving us the tools, resources, skills and strategies to help my mum and I manage.

My mum found this whole journey very overwhelming, exhausting and isolating, often describing it as like being detached from the world around her, like we were completely isolated. My mum often felt helpless and unable to understand why this was happening and how best to support me, but when the CAMHS mental health and eating disorder team, family intervention and social services support workers, autism services charities and support groups got involved, it was like we had our army by our side standing and marching alongside us to give us the space, support and understanding that we needed to manage this. They didn't give up on us. They provided us with practical and emotional skills and tools to be able to create our very own managing toolboxes, such as emotion and communication boards, grounding strategies, sensory skills and items and conversation techniques.

Coping with school was like being in a scary new world with so many new people, challenges and environments to navigate. I was in mainstream education and therefore the school had no specialities for managing autism, anxiety and mental health. However, the support of a family member being in with me in class, regular MDT (Multi Disciplinary Team) meetings with professionals, family, mental health, family and social care services became my fighters. They shouted from the rooftops what my autism and anxiety really looked like and together we created an educational toolkit with these resources in place to help me manage. Bullying was something I experienced. I wish that at that time my army could have come into school to teach others what autism, anxiety and these other conditions meant. Being educated early on can mean that we are all equipped in our own ways to understand these challenges and struggles and to know that being different from each other can be truly empowering, because by being different we can all succeed together.

Having communication boards and regular one-to-one support from teachers helped me to feel like I could share my voice. They provided me with creative learning support so that I could be taken on my own unique learning journey of discovery, which felt like an adventure. This helped to engage, inspire and empower me and gave me a feeling of belonging and inclusivity.

When I finally had my autism assessment at my local child development centre, it was like being taken into my own world. Although it was scary, as they had to ask lots of questions about me, thankfully my mum was there. They had to assess every area of my life. It made me feel like I had been really bad for this to happen but it showed that these professionals cared and wanted what was best for me. After hours of form filling, assessments and questions, we were sent away with information packs and then had to await a report and follow up meeting with the results. When they confirmed autism weeks later, it was like the weight of the world had finally been lifted; we had been heard, listened to and understood, and I realised that having a label of autism and anxiety, alongside my eating disorder and self-harm, was nothing to be ashamed of. It made me unique. I believe that all of us have our own individualities to be proud of. Having to go through this and have these diagnoses can feel scary and hard, but then a relief as it can then allow you to be equipped, aware and give you a way to understand. It is finally a way of finding yourself through that dark, long train tunnel and reaching that end destination, knowing that you are on the right pathway forward, allowing you and your child to live the best life possible and not let autism and anxiety define your lives or who you are.

My key message for you in this chapter is about building connections and fighting for early intervention if your child is going through this. Being labelled with these conditions is nothing to be ashamed of, as once you are aware of it, you can deal with it.

> "Don't think that there's a different, better child 'hiding' behind the autism. This is your child. Love the child in front of you. Encourage their strengths, celebrate their quirks, and improve their weaknesses, the way you would with any child."
> https://www.autismparentingmagazine.com/quotes-about-autism/

From what I've spoken about, I feel that some of the sites below can help to equip you with the resources, strategies, support and things to think about to help you on your journey:

https://www.autistica.org.uk/what-is-autism/what-is-autism

https://www.autistica.org.uk/what-is-autism/signs-and-symptoms/anxiety-and-autism

https://www.autism.org.uk/advice-and-guidance/topics/behaviour/meltdowns/all-audiences

https://www.autism.org.uk/advice-and-guidance/topics/mental-health/autistic-fatigue/autistic-adults

https://www.facebook.com/theicannetwork/photos/

autism-overwhelm-graphic-linkstext-the-same-activities-
that-can-cause-a-meltdown/1708979365953933/
https://www.autism.org.uk/

My final message to you is to never give up, never stop
believing, be proud of your child, build your own support
army and never let anything get in your way or hold you
back because having autism and anxiety makes us brave,
makes us bruised and makes our children who they are
meant to be. The world will be your oyster, just wait and
see.

***

*I would like to dedicate this chapter to all parents, carers and
professionals who work so hard to support their children and young
people who are finding their way through anxiety and autism. You
are true warriors, amazing and all offer something wonderful and
unique to this world.*

*I would like to dedicate this chapter to my mum, family and
friends, all the professionals in my autism, family intervention and
support services, social care services, mental health, eating disorder
team, autism specialist services and charities like Autism Guernsey,
Action for Children and Beat the UK eating disorder charity who
supported me and continue to support me as I navigate this journey
to become the Emily I am today.*

*I would like to acknowledge and thank the support of Cassie Swift
who has been absolutely amazing in supporting me, inspiring and*

*encouraging me to be able to successfully complete this chapter, I
couldn't have done it without your fantastic support.*

Emily Nuttall is a motivational disability, children,
young people, families and homelessness campaigner
and advisor with Action for Children. Emily is also an
incredible mental health and eating disorder campaigner,
champion and speaker, disability sports coach with
Guernsey Mobility Let's Go, MOE foundation coach, an
entrepreneur and inspirational co-author of the books *It's
Ok to Not Be Ok*, *Inspirational Women of the World*, *Time to
Talk Mental Health Poetry Book*, *The Children's Mental Health
Wellbeing Handbook* and she is currently writing her own
book. Emily is an active fundraiser, campaigner and media
volunteer for Beat the UK eating disorders charity, she is
a health connections community connector, Mind media
volunteer and Action for Children ambassador.

Emily is currently embarking on her counselling skills
level two to become a future counsellor, building
and developing her Motivate the Mind business and
completing her sports coaching and disability studies. She
has a background of studies in health and social care and
previous employment with children and young people
through the Guernsey Youth Commission. Emily is a
trained adult and youth mental health first aider and has
completed domestic violence awareness training.

Emily was diagnosed with cerebral palsy at the age of
one, lost the sight in her left eye at the age of eleven,

was diagnosed with scoliosis at the age of sixteen and spondylolithesis at the age of twenty-five. She is an inspirational woman who has overcome adversity. From the age of twelve, Emily has struggled with anxiety, autism, depression, self-harm, suicide, anorexia and is a domestic violence and emotional abuse survivor. She has overcome homelessness and family breakdowns and, as a previous young carer, Emily is all about empowering people and inspiring long lasting change.

https://linktr.ee/emilyn93

Listen to the audio version here:
https://bit.ly/autismandanxietydoesntdefineme

A SPIRITUAL VIEW OF ANXIETY

Julie Ferris and Karen Goodson

*"Having a parent that listens, creates a child who believes
he or she has a voice. That matters in this world."*
– Rachel Macy Stafford

To be in the energy of anxiety feels like your feet are held in
sludge, restricting your freedom, your movement.

And, as you stand still, day after day in anxiety, you may
feel like you are sinking and it becomes more difficult to
move; to do what you wish to do, to have the freedom that
your inner being desires. And, as you sink, you may feel
constricted. The energy that should flow through your
body in joy becomes stilted.

And your heart, your beautiful heart, tries to speak to
you, telling you to move the energy and help it flow. Your
body tries to entice you into movement, into expression to
help you release this energy that is pooling in your body
with no outlet.

There is a battle, and your mind is like the commander,
reinforcing the energy of anxiety, amplifying this energy.

So, how can you help yourself become unstuck? You
may like to try expressing through your voice. Through
sound. Not necessarily words but sounds to describe how

you are feeling. Let your heart give you these sounds to help you release this energy of anxiety, to bring back your flow of energy.

You may wish to sit on the ground to connect with the vibrancy and aliveness of nature. Ask for your energy to flow between you and Mother Earth. Allow the energy of the earth to flow through the soles of your feet and your hands. Intend for your energy of anxiety to be transmuted within the earth and you may find that you are able to stand and move, dance, run, hop or do a handstand. Find joy in movement. Find joy in allowing your energy to flow, allowing the energy of Mother Earth to flow through you. Whatever element you are drawn to – water, earth, air, or being close to a fire (safely) – ask for support to turn your anxiety into the natural elements of Mother Earth.

When your body moves and your energy flows, your mind will quieten. And the version of you that is dancing and moving, and flowing in energy and wisdom, can then look at the version of you who is there with the mind racing, problems weighing heavily on their shoulders. By observing what is around that version of you, your heart and your mind can assist in recognising which anxieties are truly there and those which can be released immediately. For those anxieties that are truly there, look through your heart for a solution.

Your solution may be to sing your song, to express who you are, to express your true magnificence as a soul. Or it may be to just focus on one of the earthly matters that you are juggling. Take one at a time and it may be that those other things you are juggling can just simply rest and go.

We now share the story of the fairy and the dragon. You may choose to listen to the audio version of the story, or you may choose to read it together, star children, parents, and loved ones. Some of you may like to explore together what it feels like to be the dragon or to be the fairy. Listen and allow a lightness in your heart, in play and in joy, for joy will help you to unravel and ruffle your wings to fly above earthly matters that cause you anxiety.

The Fairy and the Dragon

On this particular day, the mighty dragon was flying his usual route, across the sky, down below the hills and swooping up, stretching his wings, roaring his roar and playing with his friends in the sky.

Then the day came when the young dragon was summoned to Dragon Hill and, inside the hill, he was given his scroll of those things in life that he had always wanted to do. He opened this scroll with excitement but then saw that the list that he had made at the very beginning of his life was very, very long.

"Ooh, I don't remember writing down all these things!" he said, looking at all that he had decided to do in his dragon life:

- discover a land,
- bathe in water in the underwater city of light,
- visit many castles across the globe,
- and all the other things he had agreed to do.

And, suddenly, a little swirl of blackness gnawed at his stomach. It clawed its way to his heart, and he felt that he would be unable to do all these things, and being unable to do something as a dragon is not good. That is what they had told him.

His scales felt itchy. When he tried to roar, only a little sound came out. It was as though this black worry had taken his body prisoner, and so he sat there inside that hill, not quite knowing what he should do.

When he walked out into the sunlight, he sat on a rock, but his head was in a cloud of confusion, and his body felt paralysed. So, he sat there, and he sat there, and he sat there.

Elsewhere in that realm, the fairy felt his pain through the rock. It was her duty to tend to the rocks and the minerals to check they were feeling well and just to chat. This fairy loved to chat, and as she went around zooming through the plants, alighting on the rocks, she began to feel, in her heart, a pain coming from them. They knew what was happening, these rocks, and they showed the fairy where the pain had originated.

The fairy did not usually go beyond her home, but the rocks led her further and further and further away. As she hovered in the sky, she turned to face the green beauty of her home and she felt a little twinge of worry in her heart because she was going to fly so far away. But she sang, and her voice, her beautiful voice, calmed the twinge in her heart so that she could carry on.

And so, before long, the fairy arrived at the rock. She saw that the creature on the rock had black worry in its heart, which sank down into the rock; it flowed into the ground like a web of black fingers, and she felt the pain of the creature in her heart. Although she had never seen such a creature, for she was a young fairy, she felt that it needed some assistance from her.

So, she spoke to the creature who thought her a fly and blew her away. She tried again with her fairy song, the song that she had used to help her own heart, and the strangest thing happened. When she began to sing, the creature, the dragon on the rock, started to wiggle its toes, then its claws and its wings.

Before the creature knew what was happening, it opened its mouth and out came its roar, its voice, its song. To anybody watching, what a strange sight! A tiny fairy hovering with a beautiful song, a large dragon lifting its head and singing its song. And the sound moved that black worry from the heart of the dragon. It was blasted out through his mouth and the dragon felt a lightness as it spoke its language, as it released the worry, and fired it out, far, far away from him.

He saw the worry, like a cloud of bad weather, be blown by his song, so he sang harder and louder. The more he sang his song, the more the worry cloud was blasted away, until it was no longer there.

The joy he felt! He stood and this time he saw the fairy and they danced, singing their songs. If you've ever seen a dragon and a fairy dance, it is a most beautiful sight; and they danced and they danced, and the rocks below them danced and so did the earth. The song and the dance made a golden light, a round, shimmering light, moving between the rocks, between the friends.

This story does not end here, for the dragon and the fairy became good friends, and many adventures they had together. If you look closely, you may see one of their adventures. You may even be in one of them, you never know.

The end.

Do you feel you need help to sing your song like the dragon and the fairy? Perhaps you worry that no sound will come out or that the wrong sound will emerge. Your sound is within you.

Here is a visualisation journey you could take with an animal guide or a friend to help you find your song within you.

Imagine the most beautiful place ever. Crystal clear waters, majestic snow-topped mountains, warm, sandy deserts. Lush greenery where flowers grow, their colours dotting the landscape… maybe a beautiful cave, encrusted with crystals and gems. Or a pathway through an ancient forest.

If you wish, intend to meet a guide who will help you find your heart's song and see who comes along. You may meet a dragon friend, a fairy, dolphin, eagle, mermaid, a member of your family, or you may just have a sense of a loving presence with you, holding your hand, smiling in encouragement at you.

Walk the path, swim the waters or climb the mountain and feel your heart open, as if it were a flower. Feel where your heart draws you, as you walk, swim or move to your special place.

Your heart will guide you. Listen to your body and your heart to feel where your soul song is. Have you hidden it? Do you need to break something down to find it?

If you do, there will be a tool especially for you, so this task is easy and smooth, for the song is yours and wishes to come back to you. And when you feel you are there, be with yourself in peace and in knowing.

Is there something for you to open, like a box, to reveal your soul song? Open it. And then open your mouth, and allow your song to return, for this is who you are.

You are a most loved and valuable being. Reclaim who you are and share with others who you are, because you are a precious gift. A gift you may wish to share with certain others in your life, remaining true to your own soul song.

Whenever you feel anxious, express yourself through your song, using your voice, and moving your physical body. It is very powerful and may break down walls of worry that may not even be your walls, but walls that you have decided to stand behind.

To find your own worries, go to that place within yourself, your heart. Look at your worries through your heart and they may seem different to what you had imagined. You may be able to let them go, there and then.

So, sing your soul song often, for it is beautiful, it is you and you are a beautiful soul.

★★★

This chapter is dedicated to all uniquely gifted star children and their loved ones who find solace in connecting with their multi-dimensional soul family.

Julie Ferris and Karen Goodson are co-creators of The Gateway to the Avatar in You, a global project which aims to tackle the increase in mental health issues in uniquely gifted people, often labelled as autistic, neurodiverse or simply different.

Their channelled resources support soul alignment, spiritual awakening and the reclamation of individual sovereignty. Channelled stories and the Avatar cards help parents of star children connect with each other more deeply, enabling them to reveal their gifts and talents, thus thriving and not just surviving in this complex world.

Julie and Karen share many life experiences, including parenting their own highly sensitive, uniquely gifted

neurodiverse children, both having worked as teachers, counsellors and therapists, holding mental health, safeguarding and child protection roles for many years.

Julie and Karen offer a free discovery session to explore how they may support you and your family

https://linktr.ee/avatarinyou

Listen to the audio version here:
https://bit.ly/spiritualviewofanxiety

MINDPOWER PROFICIENCY®
TO NAVIGATE ANXIETY

Harry Mansfield

All young people deserve to know how to manage their anxiety and, like anything in life, it has to be learned. From when our children are born, they have the capacity to learn a huge number of skills and a vast extent of their talents are absorbed naturally. Learning how to manage anxiety needs awareness and practice.

MindPower Proficiency® strengthens the mind, making it agile, resilient and competent to jump into action in the correct way to tackle anxiety. Once learned, it also benefits hugely the physical side of your children's health. I have worked with a number of young people who were not aware that the headache, the pain in their stomach, their body temperature, or feeling sick was actually their anxiety. Learning these techniques also prevents mental health problems in the years to come.

Every young person's anxiety comes from a different place and their way out of it is individual to them. In this chapter are cases of young people I have worked with, which you may be able to relate to, either with your own children, or those of your family and friends.

A six-year-old boy struggling with the expectations of the education system and how to behave at school. His anxiety turned into defensive bouts of anger – both verbal and physical – threatening his place at school.

"Now I get that some things at school are not being horrible to me and it's okay I don't like them."

A fourteen-year-old girl who was bullied in the playground and struggled with friendships.

"I know now I am a bigger and stronger person than I ever thought I was."

An eleven-year-old boy whose anxiety had stopped him from enjoying sleepovers with friends and made him too scared to show parents round on school open days.

His mother later contacted me to say he had done both since working with me.

A sixteen-year-old boy in his GCSE year having increased physical symptoms as a result of his anxiety; nausea, sweats and headaches. When he vomited, he was off school for the obligatory forty-eight hours. The anxiety cycle started all over again striving to catch up on his GCSE syllabus.

"I would have thought my anxiety would have got a lot worse for my exams but in fact it got a lot better."

We will return to each case later in the chapter to show how they learned to manage – and in some cases eliminate totally – their anxieties.

Fundamentals

Anxiety is completely natural and comes in many forms. Recognising the type of anxiety, its strength and impact is paramount in ensuring a child gets through it successfully. Identifying how their mind works is key to achieving this.

Key Point

Learning a technique called ETA will allow your child to understand when anxiety is manifesting. It will stop their mind from spiralling out of control. All young people have the ability and talent to do this.

EMOTION: The feeling you feel, it is what it is, and it is completely natural, even if totally different from someone else's reaction. By recognising the emotion, either positive or challenging, your child will begin to understand where the anxiety is coming from.

THOUGHT: This is where you need to learn what to change. The mind naturally doubles up on the emotion unless it is trained not to. For example, it becomes worried about being anxious, or perhaps happy about being happy! The mind needs to be trained so the thought is simply awareness and acceptance and not amplifying the emotion. This will stop the anxiety in its tracks.

ACTION: If the thought is correct, you then act in the right way. The action is what your child does to control the anxiety rather than the anxiety controlling them.

Just Think About This!

The mind is invisible and untouchable and yet, by controlling the unseen and the untouchable, children can control their anxiety and their lives are dramatically improved.

The mind controls the brain so, if you are looking to give your child the skills to curb their anxiety, they need to learn MindPower Proficiency®: the power to control the mind, which in turn controls the brain and body.

When you train and strengthen the mind, it changes how the brain adjusts your thoughts, your memory, your emotions, your touch, your breathing, your temperature and every process that regulates anxiety.

MindPower Proficiency® changes mental processes, thoughts, consciousness, actions and consequently anxiety.

When learning anything, practice is the key to moving forward. This is particularly important as your mind is changing constantly, both subconsciously and consciously, and at great speed.

The Transformation Triangle® – Point One

When training, I use my registered behaviour model, 'The Transformation Triangle®', to train the mind and control anxiety. Firstly, young people have to be *aware* of how their mind is reacting, then *challenge* their mind, along with the others around them, to put the correct action in place. They can *transform* the outcome from their anxiety into a positive experience. This method teaches young people how to ACT in a way that works for them and their anxiety.

Being under pressure is part of life and it is essential for young people to use what is around them to help when anxiety manifests itself. Controlling their anxiety will come in many forms.

The Transformation Triangle® – Point Two

Each person reading this will learn in a different way and enjoy different things, and we learn the most when we are doing the things that we get pleasure from. Sport may thrill a person or make them feel uncomfortable. Animals may relax or worry someone. Nature may ease tension when in it or it could bore you to tears! Whatever the reaction, learning to use them as a successful tool to control anxiety is priceless and incalculable in a young person's life. These tools can then be taken on into adulthood.

SPORT: Sports people manage anxiety both personally and within a team. When learning any sport, a key part is training the mind; to use the conscious mind in the correct way in order for the subconscious mind to work successfully, calmly and without anxiety.

A tennis player, when learning to serve, has to use their

mind and body consecutively 100,000 times to achieve the measured winning movement. Their mind is then able to successfully get the body to serve correctly in the same way that the mind can be trained to effectively manage anxiety.

ANIMALS: Their reaction shows what the emotion is and how it is affecting you. Without a speaking voice, they communicate in a very different way, which we can learn a great deal from to strengthen the mind. Working with them using MindPower Proficiency®, the young person becomes aware of their ETA (Emotion, Thought, Action) and their levels of calmness versus their anxiety in any given situation.

NATURE: When in nature, our senses come to the fore, and when using each of them in turn, and amalgamating them with testing our mind, we alter the processes of the mind and anxiety. In nature, we have the time and space to analyse. Learning from nature's framework gives us essential skills for navigating anxiety.

The Transformation Triangle® – Point Three

A child's awareness of what their mind is doing is paramount to recognising anxiety in its numerous forms and often, as with adults, the subconscious takes over and this key objective is missed. Identifying the cause and effect it has on themselves and their surroundings is key in absorbing the necessary information for the child to know what to do regarding moving forward. Without this training, huge health repercussions develop further down the line.

It is essential for any young person – or, for that matter, any adult because of our ability to influence our children hugely – to know that a mental and physical reaction comes in so many different forms, individual to each child. Initially this awareness of what the young person's mind is doing and how the anxiety is manifesting physically as a result of their mind can be hard to grasp but, without it, the mind spirals out of control.

The cause and effect from each situation can be due to a number of factors, such as environment, company, a given task and so much more. Each changes the mind and therefore the level of anxiety.

An absolute necessity in life is moving forward and anxiety must not be allowed to take hold to prevent your child from doing just that. Once awareness and acceptance have been validated, the cause and effect on the mind, body and surroundings recognised allows the method of moving forward to be decided.

Illustrations

We will return now to the four young people mentioned at the beginning of this chapter. Below is a brief outline of how they learned to train their minds to be more powerful and proficient when their anxiety struck.

Six-year-old boy:
Analysing himself without judgement, and this is key, he wanted one of our dogs' friendship but found that he had to allow the relationship with the dog to be a two-way conversation to get the friendship. When reflecting, he realised that when he was at school he had taken over relationships, other children got cross, and his behaviour escalated in the wrong way. It was easy for him to see the dog's behaviour change from his behaviour; when he was angry the dog became more tense and edgy.

Similarly, to be safe with dogs, there are rules of how to behave, which he translated to school life and the rules they have in place to keep him and the other children safe.

When learning how to put news skills in place, it wasn't instantly learned, but the awareness of the effect that he had on what was happening at school was instant.

Eleven-year-old boy:
Nature gave this boy the time to feel and work out where his anxiety was coming from and what reaction his body had from it. His life was fast paced with high expectations. Suitable exercises and being given the space to learn at his natural pace allowed him to work out the cause of his anxiety and its effect on him. From this, we created a way for him to move forward.

We used the senses that worked for him and paused on many occasions to acquire the techniques that would work for him. The anxiety which had completely taken away his happiness and joy had gone, he had grown stronger and was having fun again.

Fourteen-year-old girl:

In this case, the girl chose to work mainly with the horses. Her difficult experiences at school had left her feeling incredibly judged and the pony she chose to work with has a very independent temperament!

She wanted interaction with the pony, but the pony regularly wanted her own space, denying her the desired attention, conversation and interaction. She quickly learned that she had done nothing to upset the pony at all and discovered that if someone doesn't want you to be part of their crowd it is important to realise that it is their decision and not to take it personally. She then had the power whether or not to pursue this kind of relationship and that she had control of the anxiety it caused her.

Sixteen-year-old boy:

When a young person has a very quick mind it is harder for them to accept and understand that what is happening around them isn't going to happen at their pace. Endless tensions and anxieties had crept in causing his body to become tired and exhausted as it couldn't keep up with his mind.

He is a particularly sporty young man, so it was clear that through sport he was going to be able to understand his mind. He already knew that he had to train his body for the sports he played – to become stronger and more agile.

Training the mind then seemed to make sense whereas before it had sounded ridiculous!

Through the sport we played, the young man slowly recognised the changes in his mind and body and how to improve. Recognising faulty sports techniques that needed to be corrected, he then discovered how his mind was becoming calmer and stronger with the work.

Summary

This short chapter is just the tip of the iceberg. We all have to start somewhere when learning a new skill and these techniques are the foundation for your child to stop their anxiety in its tracks through learning how to have a powerful and proficient mind.

★★★

Dedicated to William and Marcus whom I have watched grow into amazing young men using these skills to navigate their anxieties with great success.

Harry Mansfield has become affectionately known as "The MindPower Champion" through her excellent understanding of how advantageous it is when you have the skills to know how your mind works and having further techniques for strength and success through the use of your mind.

She first realised how powerful the mind can be when training to parachute over thirty years ago. This, along with being a sports coach for twenty-five years, a life-changing head injury and adversity as a child, led her to set up the only online and in person training system for clients to learn how to have a strong and proficient mind by teaching "MindPower Proficiency®".

Her work as a Mental Strength Consultant shows that training the mind for mental strength is the foundation for absolutely everything we do. Her training company, The Awareness Key, teaches her registered behaviour model "The Transformation Triangle", how to be Aware of the mind, Challenge it and Transform it – ACT.

https://linktr.ee/harrymansfield

Listen to the audio version here:
https://bit.ly/mindpowerproficiency

STORY FOLLOWS STATE

Healing your nervous system will change the way you view the world

Laura Linklater

> *"Much of what we call personality is not a fixed set of traits, only coping mechanisms a person acquired in childhood."*
>
> – *Gabor Maté*

Parenting is as tough as it is rewarding. There are a million books, blogs, social media accounts and stories from tired, stressed mums, dads and carers the world over that show you are not alone in having challenging days!

Any career that involves working with children will take you on a similar roller coaster of epic highs and deep lows with how you feel about your ability as a supporter of children and how you respond or react to their often challenging, and usually developmentally appropriate behaviour.

Put succinctly: our kids trigger us.

Children's behaviour can tap into our deep *emotional triggers* from our own early experiences (as we wonder, 'Am

I good enough?' 'Am I smart enough?' 'Did I mess them up forever with that interaction?') and our perfectly normal *environmental triggers*, such as tiredness and overwhelm as we spin a million plates simultaneously, hunger, chronic dehydration, and so on.

The adult experience of stress in any adult–child relationship is an incredibly important component to the interactions they share. We feel our reaction to children's behaviour deep in our bodies. Think of your body state last time you were stressed out or anxious (no matter the source of the stress):

- Shoulders rise
- Back muscles tense
- Your stomach twists and flips
- Your facial muscles freeze
- Breath comes faster, and inhales are shallower

All of this is a normal and healthy response to a threat. The threat can be real (as in a car not slowing as you step onto the zebra crossing), or it can be a perceived threat (such as when you have an exam and you're worried about the possibility of failing it or the ramifications of not hitting your projected grades).

Research into Polyvagal Theory strongly demonstrates that 'story follows state'. This means that your thoughts about a situation are informed by your body's reaction to the initial event. Your physical response comes first, followed by the story we tell ourselves... and then you act on the story your mind constructs.

To more fully understand this, we need to look a bit closer at the very nature of human beings. What are we really? We are mammals. Yes, human beings have these incredible supercomputer brains, capable of complex language, forward thinking, past reminiscing and making lightning-fast intelligent connections unlike any other animal on this planet. But we are also, at base, mammals.

Your mammal body is primed for two things during your lifetime: survival and passing on genetic material by raising the next generation. The drive to survive throughout human evolution has led to the incredibly fine alert systems built into the body – through the vagus nerve – to protect you and ensure you live as long as possible. Your body and brain are constantly scanning your environment for potential threats you need to respond to.

As social animals, this threat perception also includes how others interact with us, as the mind scans for possible signs of rejection, or social misunderstanding. To the early human, ostracisation from the group may well have been an extremely dangerous, even fatal, fate. Unfortunately, our mammal bodies still react to these ancient dangers on a primitive level.

If you have ever had the experience of not being in control of a huge wave of anger, fear or anxiety in a situation with your children, the chances are your nervous system was being triggered by an *emotional wound* or *environmental stressor*. Your threat perception mechanism was mobilised for your own protection. In Polyvagal Theory, this is referred to as a *neuroception*. It is so normal, there is an actual term for it – you are not alone by any stretch.

The process of neuroception, which occurs below our conscious awareness, could look like you jumping at a loud bang, even though you know it is most likely something innocuous. Here, we gain a deeper understanding of veterans struggling with the sound of fireworks, or footage of entire shopping malls full of people in the USA skittering in hysteria because they mistook a motorcycle backfiring for their deepest fear: the active shooter scenario.

It could also be linked to your developmental experiences. In my work with Cycle Breaker Parents, I have supported clients with understanding and healing their nervous system, which was primed and calibrated in survival mode through their challenging childhood. The parent or carer – and I include professionals who work with children here – who experienced an adult shouting and screaming at them will experience a child screaming at them as a neuroception for danger. The body will prime a response against what it learned was a threat behaviour from another, which is how adults who wish to be calm and gentle in their relationships find themselves reacting with anger or drawing away physically or emotionally from a situation. The primal drive for safety takes over and your mammal brain floods your body with hormones that guide your behaviour.

So, what if the body's defence mechanisms are not serving you in your current circumstances?

You are now a grown adult. You are not a powerless child or young person in a stressful environment. You want to respond to your children's inner needs, as expressed by their outward behaviours, with gentle guidance as you support them to move through their feelings and learn to regulate themselves.

There are a number of skills that you can learn in order to help you to support the children and young people in your life with their big feelings and coping mechanisms. Hopefully by now you are also seeing that devoting some time and energy towards befriending and healing your nervous system is just as important as learning yet more skills or phrases to say when a child is struggling.

A short introduction to Polyvagal Theory

Polyvagal Theory has been around since Dr Stephen Porges PhD first presented it in 1994, following decades of research. The insights gained by his team furthered our knowledge into the ways in which the strength of the vagus nerve supports the survival and thriving of newborn babies.

Since the late 1990s, Polyvagal Theory has been applied in the therapeutic context, particularly with those who have experienced trauma, by leading Polyvagal Therapist Deb Dana and Dr Mona Delahooke, who has masterfully integrated Polyvagal Theory in her work in understanding the behaviour of children and young people. My own work, Polyvagal Parenting, will be released towards the end of 2022.

The Vagus Nerve

Polvagal Theory centres around the vagus nerve, which travels through the body from the brain stem, behind the heart and lungs and down to the diaphragm. Vagus means 'wandering' – as the vagrant. The vagus nerve, as found in modern-day humans, has evolved in three separate stages, all of which are responsible for differing levels of protection mechanism activation in our mammal bodies.

The lower, middle and upper parts of the vagus nerve are often depicted as three parts of a ladder, since activation of each area is characterised by very different safety responses.

Ventral Vagal

The 'top of the ladder', so to speak, is, in terms of the evolution of the human body and protective systems, the most recent addition. This is where humans feel they are safe to connect with others, and it is part of what has made us successful as a socially co-ordinated species.

When you are in the ventral vagal state, your social engagement system is active. This means you enjoy being with other people and you are able to communicate your own needs and thoughts – and reliably interpret others' body language as you navigate social encounters.

The body is able to 'rest and digest', with healthy heart function, regular blood pressure and a healthy immune system being enabled. You are likely to describe yourself as feeling safe, calm, happy and interested in what is going on around you. Thoughts are organised and taking care of yourself feels easy to do.

Put simply, the ventral vagal stage is a great place to be – and it's where we would like our children to be much of the time too.

Sympathetic Nervous System – alert

When a neuroception for 'unsafe' activates the sympathetic nervous system (SNS), the body enters fight or flight mode and switches from 'safe to connect' to 'alert for danger'. Outwardly, you may be behaving in the same way. Internally, the body and the mind are mobilising for safety and preparing you to act.

When the SNS is aroused, you are likely to describe yourself as anxious, alert, hypervigilant and feel the need to move and take action. Sounds that may have seemed friendly before are suddenly scrutinised for duplicity or sharpness and your attention may feel split, making it harder to focus on tasks.

Longer term issues related to living in the SNS state for prolonged periods include high blood pressure, irregular sleep patterns, headaches, digestive discomfort, memory or concentration struggles and decreased immune system function.

This state serves us well when there is a threat that we need to respond to, but it is not healthy to exist entirely or mostly in this state.

Dorsal Vagal – The bottom of the ladder

This is the oldest and most primitive of the three vagal pathways. It is seen throughout the animal kingdom as a base-level response to threat: shut down and play dead until the threat has passed.

The dorsal vagal state in humans accounts for the dissociative state that many report when their mind and their nervous system is overwhelmed. People in the dorsal state report feeling lost, lonely, hopeless. Cognitive function becomes slower, leading to brain fog, memory impairment and a feeling that the world is a dark, empty place where no one understands.

Living in this vagal state for long periods has been linked to chronic stomach/digestion problems, fatigue, weight gain and fibromyalgia. Often, support is required to enable someone in the dorsal vagal state to climb back up the ladder.

The daily dance

You move up and down the ladder multiple times a day, depending on your internal and external realities: perhaps someone says something unkind and you move from ventral vagal to SNS. You land a great deal at work and you move up a few rungs from SNS to ventral vagal. Engaging in a soothing activity, such as yin yoga, could support you to gently climb out of dorsal vagal despair and towards SNS by adding movement through your body.

Why Polyvagal Theory is so empowering

Befriending your nervous system so that you are able to identify which stage you are in at a given moment is incredibly powerful. You are then able to go further and use Polyvagal Therapy techniques, or create your own personal ones, to help you move through the states in a conscious, mindful manner.

This empowers you to work with your nervous system in order to create the reality you both desire and deserve. It is not possible – nor is it adaptive – to live our entire lives in ventral vagal activation. There will be times when your SNS is required to support you in taking action to move you to safety quickly, and there will be life events (such as the loss of a loved one or upsetting world events) that will result in a visit to the dorsal vagal state.

Understanding Polyvagal Theory – and your personal lived experience of the interplay of the three states – is crucial in regaining your power to find your own peace in your own time, without being reliant upon external factors (such as another person/approval of others/substances, etc.). It also enables you to tune into the wisdom of each stage and to be a full participant in your own life.

Your nervous system is moving through these states constantly, whether you are aware of it or not. Becoming conscious of this process can be a powerful catalyst for change, not only in your life, but in your relationships.

As you become aware of this in yourself, you will be able to witness the quest for survival as it is happening for those around you – most especially your children. You will be more able to respond consciously and calmly to their needs and to guide them with compassion and confidence.

★★★

To my children who not only show me the areas in which I can heal and love my inner child self more deeply, but also treat me with grace and kindness as I grow and learn with them. I am so honoured to walk this winding path of life with you. Thank you. All my love.

Laura is a cycle-breaker parent mentor. She helps parents who had a tough upbringing and are committed to being the gentle, empowering parent they always dreamed they would be.

Laura is on a mission to support and guide conscious parents as they heal and learn practical skills so that they can in turn support their child/ren's emotional and behavioural development.

Laura helps you to identify and honour your triggers for reactions in ways you don't wish to act in your role as parent (shouting, anger, shaming, withdrawing), to make sense of your past experiences and to find peace as you embark on your journey of self-healing.

She also helps you to understand your child's behaviour and teaches you practical parenting, listening and conflict resolution skills you need so you can raise up your child/ren and break the cycles you do not wish to pass on.

Laura helps parents to break their cycles so that they can support their children to flourish, and build a connected, loving family.

Healing + skills = the parent you always wanted to be!

https://linktr.ee/cyclebreakerparents

Listen to the audio version here:
https://bit.ly/storyfollowsstate

MUM GUILT

You are not alone in navigating the relentless grip of shame

Jo Picken

Guilt and shame associated with motherhood can seep into every part of our lives and, according to a study by NUK, almost 90% of mums feel that guilt and shame every day! EVERY DAY!

Brené Brown talks about the:

> *"Places we go when we fall short; Shame [and] Guilt*
> *Shame – I am bad … Flawed and unworthy.*
> *Guilt – I did something bad. Discomfort we feel when …*
> *we've failed."*

Brown, 2021

Why, as mums, do we always think and feel we are not enough?

Mum guilt is the guilt that mothers carry with them day in, day out, for a lifetime. You have heard of it. You have probably experienced it. We all know that it can totally ruin your day, your week, your year and even the time you spend with your precious children.

One little mistake, an accident, a spilt drink, a snap of being short-tempered, a day of screens, a stop at McDonald's, the choice to use baby formula or when to wean, going back to work, not going back to work, an unexpected trip to A&E (those moments always happen when you turn your back for one second), arguments with your teens, no one helping out around the house.

Sound familiar?

All these experiences can send a normally relaxed and awesome mum reeling into the "guilt zone", and the guilt zone can easily spiral into negative self-talk.

When the negative self-talk starts, it often sounds like:

- What if I'm doing everything wrong?
- What if my kids don't turn out okay?
- What if they grow up to hate me?
- What if they are not healthy?
- What if they are not meeting their potential?
- What if they need therapy when they are older?

Mums carry an enormous responsibility in life, from the moment of conception, which no one prepares them for.

Most mums value their children above almost everything in the world, but they also slip up, which feels like mistakes, they get tired, they cry, they get angry, they buy fast food, they get overwhelmed, they definitely need a break, they don't do the cleaning, they also leave washing in the machine and re-wash it more times than they admit to. They question everything and once upon a time they had interests and passions outside of parenting. Mums are human. You are human and a blinking amazing one at that!

Does this all sound like you?

Have you been suffering from a heavy dose of mum guilt?

Is it keeping you from thinking you could be the best mum in the world?

Are you tired of feeling ashamed and guilty all the time?

This chapter of the book is aimed at helping you work through what mum guilt is and how to manage it in a healthy way.

Mum Guilt, What Is It All About?

Mum guilt is an overwhelming feeling that you are failing in some way; a feeling you just cannot shake. You may have anxieties about how your kids are developing or who they will be when they grow up and you may feel like any problems that arise are entirely your fault. You may worry that they will resent you as adults or need therapy to overcome their childhood and that it will be ALL your fault too.

Another symptom of mum guilt is feeling like you cannot make the right decisions for your kids – no matter what you do. When you do finally make a decision, you second-guess yourself and you are left wondering if you are doing the right thing all along.

You may dwell on past mistakes, becoming ashamed or defeated when you remember things you felt that you did wrong.

Mum guilt can be mild or severe and those with severe mum guilt may even struggle with a lack of self-confidence as a mother and in wider aspects of life too.

The Comparison Game

Mums are great at this – comparing themselves to others. Mums regularly feel guilty, just by comparing themselves to other mums. Mums they don't even know!

For example:

- Other mums always look perfect on the school run.
- Other mums feed their kids healthy, organic, home-cooked meals every night.
- Other mums effortlessly run their kids to all their activities every night of the week.
- Other mums never lose their tempers and scream blue murder at their kids.
- Other mums are always calm.
- Other mums are better than me!

What Do Mums Feel Guilty About?

Mum guilt can stem from many sources, but some common reasons us mums feel guilty are:

1. Choosing how to feed their baby.
New mums are often told of the many benefits of breastfeeding – "breast is best" rhetoric is still a strong voice. A mum who cannot or chooses not to breastfeed has

made the right choice for them and their baby, but they may feel guilty whatever the decision.

2.   Not losing weight after having a baby.
Many women have an expectation that they need to look and weigh the same as they did before having children. Not being able to fit into pre-pregnancy clothes can be a source of shame and embarrassment, which is often commented on by others close to them. In reality, a woman's body goes through an immense change when they birth new life, it's something to be celebrated, not be ashamed of.

3.   Having a home that is a tip.
Many mums struggle with guilt of having a home that isn't perfect. If they take time to clean the house, they feel like they are neglecting their children. If they take time to spend with their children, they feel like they are neglecting the housework. Then, as the kids grow, some mums feel like they are the only ones who clean up. Resentment sets in and then one day it all becomes too much. Mum snaps = more guilt.

4.   Feeding kids "junk" food.
Mums know that it's their job to feed their kids healthy and nutritious meals but pre-packaged food and take aways are just easier when life gets busy or overwhelming. Many mums feel the guilt when they compare themselves to other mums who "never go through the drive through" or "only feed their children organic, home-cooked meals".

5. Too much screen time.

Screen time is another thing that can send mums into the throes of guilt. Parents are told to limit screen time, but screens are all around and can be almost inescapable. Plus, kids TV, a tablet or a video game can give us mums some time to make a cuppa, get dinner on or do a load of washing.

6. Meltdowns at the supermarket or other public places.

Kids of any age can throw a tantrum anytime, anywhere. Mums often feel guilty, ashamed and embarrassed when it happens in public. This can be made a whole lot worse when a bystander makes a comment or says something negative about their parenting.

7. Not enough time to spend with their kids.

Busy or working mums may feel that they are not spending enough time with their kids, torn between working and being present in your children's lives.

8. Anger or impatience.

Many mums feel guilty when they raise their voices or become angry with their children. We all know we need to take a breath, pause and respond calmly, but life isn't always "positive parenting".

9. Saying the wrong thing.

Mums often wonder if they have said or done the right thing when it comes to parenting. It can be especially tricky when they are trying to discipline their child. When kids get older, mums can tear themselves apart about giving the right advice to their young adults, fearing the result not being the ideal outcome.

10. Sending them to the right school.

Especially now, in this post-lockdown world, many parents wonder if they are sending their kids to the right school. Would it be better if they sent their kids to private school? Should they try home-schooling? And knowing that no matter what you choose it could be wrong.

11. Not being able to protect them from everything.

Parents often feel guilty when a child gets sick or hurt, wondering if there was something that they could have done to prevent it. Then, as they grow, parents must stand by and watch people emotionally hurt our children – friendships break down and relationships end; it can be heart-breaking.

12. Not having enough money.

Mums can feel guilty when they cannot provide their children with the things that they desire, the things that other kids are able to have.

Financial comparisons can be hard on mums when they feel like they are not able to provide the same lifestyle.

Going to work. Not going to work. The balance between work and home, need and desire is a strong battle. Add in the guilt that some mums feel around not contributing to the family income and phew, that's a lot to deal with!

13. Being too much like their own parents.

If someone feels like their parents did a poor job raising them, they may feel guilty when what comes out of their own mouths sounds just like their own parents. Oh, the shame – it's mortifying!

And the extra one for luck, the one that really hits us hard:

14. Making mistakes.

One of the most common sources of mum guilt is making mistakes or feeling like we have made mistakes. Forgetting stuff, misunderstanding stuff, punishing a child out of a snap reaction and not backing down, accidentally missing important stuff, being late for the school run. These little slip-ups can make a mum feel awful and send her straight to the "guilt zone".

How many of them resonate with you? Be honest now…

Why Do Mums Feel Guilty?

Wow, that was one hell of a list about what mums feel guilty about, but why do mums hold on to so much guilt? Why is it normal for so many mums to feel like they are not doing enough or that they are failing their kids, daily?

Mums are prone to holding on to guilty feelings, even when they are trying their absolute best.

There are very high expectations for mums; most would agree it's for a good reason. Parents are responsible for feeding, clothing, nurturing, educating, cleaning, loving, disciplining, playing with and keeping their children safe. That is quite a responsibility!

As a mum, you are charged with such an incredible task – raising a *whole human being*, maybe more than one!

At the same time, mums are not perfect, no matter how much we wish they could be. Mums make mistakes, have hard days, say the wrong thing sometimes. Mums lose their patience, cry and get angry sometimes.

Guilt often comes from limiting beliefs, which hold us back and cloud our view of ourselves and the world around us. This is fuelled by the loud voices in our family, society or even your own internal voice placing the burden of guilt on you.

It's important to remember that NO mum is ever going to do EVERYTHING right. Please remember that those mums you are comparing yourself to are not all perfect, either. When looking at a perfect Instagram family, you never really know what's going on under the surface; they also make mistakes, burn dinner, lose their temper, and wonder if they are doing things right, just like you!

Mum; Stop Comparing Yourself

Sometimes comparison can be an awesome way to help you be better. But comparing yourself to other mums can leave you feeling guilty, embarrassed, or defensive. When comparisons make you feel ashamed, they are no longer productive.

News flash: the Insta mums who seem to have the perfect family have the same struggles in life as everyone else. Their kids argue, they make mess and have meltdowns, you just don't get shown that side of their life because those mums don't want to show you the times that they lose their temper, make mistakes and burn dinner too.

Of course, use other mums to inspire you, but avoid allowing it to cross over into a comparison battle that makes you feel bad about yourself.

Take it Easy on Yourself, Mumma

If you are sitting on your sofa, reading this and feeling bad, just remember: the mum from the film *ET* had a kid who faked being sick and had an alien living in her house for days, before she even noticed. You're definitely doing better than her!

Maybe now you have a smile on your face. Please listen when I tell you that you are doing better than okay! Be kind to your kids but, most importantly, be kind to YOU. Try not to let the weight of mum guilt crush your soul.

You are doing the best you can with the knowledge and resources you have right now!

You've got this, Mum – you are amazing!

★★★

To all mums, my mum and her mum! You are all amazing.

Jo Picken is The Holistic Business Coach, a teacher, trainer, mentor and confidence coach – she loves nothing more than to see people shine brightly, brimming with confidence.

As of 2022, Jo is a master emotional freedom technique trainer of trainers (EFT / tapping) and neuro-linguistic programming (NLP) practitioner, Usui reiki master, angelic reiki master / teacher – but, before this, she worked in education, as a teacher, for twenty years.

Her first experience of EFT and NLP happened when her life suddenly changed, and she struggled to overcome the issues this change had caused. To help herself recover, Jo delved deep into both modalities and went on to learn and qualify in the techniques that helped her on the road to emotional recovery.

Now her passion is supporting well-being practitioners and therapists (mainly mums) to develop their businesses' foundations, shine on social media and to grow in confidence to reach their goals!

Joanna Picken BA/BSC, PGDip, QTS, Cert ED

https://linktr.ee/Jopicken

Listen to the audio version here:
https://bit.ly/Mumguilt

Lightning Source UK Ltd.
Milton Keynes UK
UKHW021423220922
409272UK00005B/120